SALVAGE

SQUADRON

303

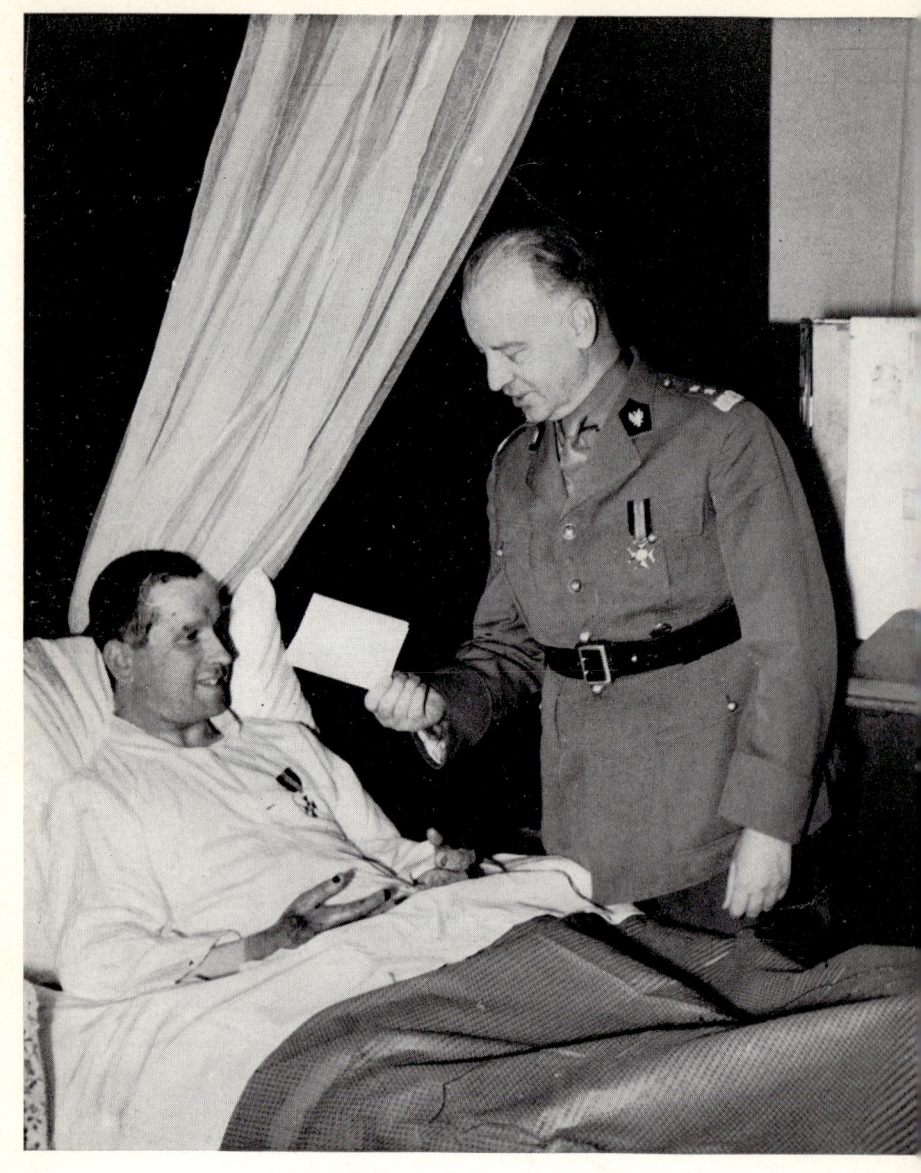

General Sikorski honors

ARKADY FIEDLER

SQUADRON 303

The Story of
The Polish Fighter Squadron
with the R.A.F.

1943

ROY, PUBLISHERS, NEW YORK

Copyright, 1943
by ROY, PUBLISHERS, A. N. New York

First Printing, February 1943
Second Printing, June 1943

PRINTED AND BOUND IN THE U. S. A. BY
KINGSPORT PRESS, INC., KINGSPORT, TENN.

"... SINCE THE DAY when Polish soldiers on foreign soil took up the arms which—for a time only—had been struck from the hands of the Nation, they have fought so well that they have won renown and glory throughout the world. I can assure you that they will continue so to fight in the future, until final victory . . ."

> GENERAL WLADYSLAW SIKORSKI,
> Commander in Chief of the Polish
> Armed Forces, speaking to Poles
> in Detroit, Mich., April 1941

CONTENTS

CHAPTER		PAGE
1.	"I AM DELIGHTED"	13
2.	THE BATTLE OF BRITAIN, 1940	23
3.	COMRADESHIP	30
4.	THE FIGHTER PILOT	40
5.	ALL BULLETS SPENT	46
6.	UPS AND DOWNS	55
7.	BIG GAME: DORNIERS	65
8.	SUFFERING	74
9.	JAN DONALD SMILES THREE TIMES	81
10.	THE CLOUD	88
11.	THE BEST SCORE	95
12.	THE ENEMY'S DANSE MACABRE	104
13.	A GALLANT CZECH, SERGEANT FRANTISEK	110
14.	THE GREY ROOTS OF BRILLIANT FLOWERS	120
15.	SANS PEUR ET SANS REPROCHE	131
16.	THE MYTH OF THE MESSERSCHMITT 110	138

CONTENTS

CHAPTER	PAGE
17. STRATAGEMS	146
18. HUMAN DESTINY HANGS IN THE BALANCE	151
19. THE BALANCE TIPS	164
20. "WE ARE BEGINNING TO UNDERSTAND THE POLES"	173

ILLUSTRATIONS

	FACING PAGE
General Sikorski honors	*frontis.*
"I am delighted"	16
". . . owed by so many to so few"	17
The victors return	32
Scoreboard	33
Uhlan rides to war	64
. . . modest, smiling	65
Like a shot partridge	80
Like hostile arrows	81
Swapping tales	112
Cherished respite	113
Barring gremlins	128
Three United Nations	129
Tallying up	160
Precious flower: comradeship	161
Raring to go	176
Like other men . . . laughs	177

SQUADRON

303

1

"I AM DELIGHTED"

It is the last day of August 1940, six o'clock in the evening. The Polish Fighter Squadron 303 is up, patrolling the outskirts of London. It is their last training flight. Tomorrow the squadron will appear on the Fighter Command operational map and take part in the Battle of Britain which has now been raging for three weeks. For three weeks the Polish fighter pilots have been counting the days, eager to be in the thick of the fight.

The sky is blue and the reddish evening sun casts a golden glow on the countryside. England, twenty thousand feet below, looks like a dreamland of peace and quiet, basking happily in the mild sunshine of late summer. The beautiful England of August! The Polish airmen yield to England's charm—and dream of coming battles.

Squadron Leader K., an Englishman, is a short and rather plump man with an apparently jovial expression. He is a splendid fighter pilot and had shot down seven German planes in France, but today there is something on his mind. He has been in charge of the Polish squadron for only a few weeks and he has some doubts about the men, though he shares his command with a Polish squadron leader. He feels a little uneasy and he sometimes wishes he had a plain, straightforward squadron of British boys to lead into the battle. How, he wonders, will the Poles stand up to their task? Apparently they have fought in Poland and in France. They are not at all bad fellows, but the squadron leader cannot help wondering why these strange and unknown pilots from Central Europe have been entrusted with one of the most vital sectors—in fact the most important of all— the defense of the Metropolis itself. Probably a case of inter-allied courtesy. But wasn't this rather overdoing it?

London is there on the left, a huge patch of gray. Even on the sunniest day a haze of smoke and mist hangs over the city. Above the haze emerge the swollen bodies of the barrage balloons, rosy in the setting sun. But the Squadron Leader does not enjoy the beauty of his England. He looks down on London and thinks of the morrow and of the days to come. If only he could know how the Poles will work. . . .

Twelve minutes past six. A voice croaks in the earphones. It is an order from the ground.

"Squadron 303, Flight A, course 90 degrees!"

Now what's up? A new maneuver? Six machines break away from the formation and fly east, in the appointed direction, under Squadron Leader K.

Soon there is a new order: "Course 100 degrees!" It sounds rather well, like the promise of real business. The five pilots following the squadron leader are thrilled. Perhaps it's beginning? . . . Then comes a sharp order: "Course 140 degrees!" No doubt about it, they are leading them on. Probably towards the enemy.

Indeed, after a few minutes they see, far away, slightly to the left, a formation of German bombers. The bombers are flying towards France, obviously returning from a raid, for one or two are trailing a little smoke. Behind and above, as usual, flies the escort of a score of Messerschmitts.

Without hesitation the flight goes into attack. It is in a good position, flying out of the sun. It has to cut across the path of the bombers before they leave England. The pilots are filled with enthusiasm. At last they will have a whack at the Germans! . . .

They had their whack, but not in the way they had hoped for. They did not reach the bombers. They were still about two miles away when three Messerschmitt 109's appeared out of the blue a few hundred yards in front of them. Three German fighters lagging behind their main formation. By a queer coincidence they failed to notice the Polish flight: coming up in a broad curve, the Germans had the Hurricanes below them, and hidden by their own wings. Moreover the flight was dead in line with the blinding sun.

The Squadron Leader, and Sergeants Szaposzka and Kar,* leap at them like a flash. The three get on the three Germans' tails, each choosing his man. The Germans are still unaware of their existence. At a distance of a hundred yards the squadron leader opens fire and in a moment the middle

---

* All the names in this book are fictitious. The true names will be given in post-war editions.

"I am delighted"

". . . owed by so many to so few"

Messerschmitt catches fire, giving the flight a grand spectacle. The German machine explodes and drops like an enormous torch; a comet with a red tail.

The other two Germans save themselves by a sudden turn, and dive. But the Sergeants are as swift in the attack. They cling to the enemy like leeches. Szaposzka, in a fantastic, almost vertical dive, calculates exactly the angle, and calmly aims below his opponent's fuselage so that he has to pass through a stream of bullets. The heavy fire acts as though tearing the entrails out of a living body.

Meantime Kar in his dive keeps right on top of the third Messerschmitt. Not firing. He waits. And watches. When at last the German begins to pull out of the dive, the sergeant is right on his back, like a vulture. At close range he fires three short bursts into the engine and the top of the cockpit, and the enemy, a streak of dense smoke, crashes to the ground.

The encounter and the destruction of the three Messerschmitts lasted only a few seconds, less time than it takes to describe. But during those few seconds another drama was enacted behind the backs of the victorious section, and Squadron Leader K. had no idea that his life had hung by a thread.

While he and his two Poles were attacking the German marauders, three more Messerschmitts came suddenly to the rescue of their comrades. They opened fire at a distance to drive off the attackers. Their fire was without effect. Besides, they had come too late, for the first three machines were already doomed.

In their blind frenzy the rescuers made a capital error: they neglected the two Polish fighters guarding the rear of the flight. As if the Hurricanes were not there, the Germans flashed past them, a blurred vision of black crosses rushing into battle. The rearguard, Pilot Officer Ox and Sergeant Zycz, went instantly full boost after them. In this furious pursuit the machines drew a complicated pattern: in front were three Germans in flames, behind them Squadron Leader K.'s section, then three more Germans, and finally a couple of Poles.

The second section of German machines was just coming within effective range of the squadron leader and Szaposzka, when the two rearguard pilots caught up with them. Ox went for the right-hand, Zycz for the left-hand machine. They fired almost simultaneously and with identical results: mortally wounded, the two Messerschmitts plunged downward, one emitting billows of smoke, the other a great mass of flame. The third seized the opportunity to slip off.

A nice scrum! Five German machines sent down, an evil omen for the enemy. Two Jerries baled out, the others perished in the flames and wreckage of their planes. A victory all the more remarkable because it had been achieved so easily, with so little effort. It was the best type of team-work, a clean game well played.

And overwhelming, too. The Polish pilots were amazed. These Hurricanes! What a thrill to be wielding this incomparable instrument! Its eight machine-guns had an incredibly crushing fire power.

All the pilots but one had had their share in the success. The sixth man, Pilot Officer Dzidek, the leader of the second section, had a victorious private adventure of his own a little later. Seeing the break-up of the first three Messerschmitts and knowing nothing of the fight in which his two companions were engaged behind him, he wagged his wings, signalling them to follow, and flew off to where in the distance he saw four other Messerschmitts. They were about two thousand yards away and seemed strangely nervous. They were all making maneuvers to avoid attack. Dzidek caught them up easily, and only then realized that he was alone, without his companions.

He did not retreat. Whatever happened, he was determined to get his Jerry too. An old hand at the game, he did not rush into a headlong, suicidal attack. He took up a good position a few hundred yards above and behind the four Messerschmitts, shadowing them patiently, mile after mile. A hungry wolf following a flock.

They crossed the major part of Kent and approached the coast. The Germans, although they had superiority in numbers, had no desire to fight. They seemed rather to be fleeing in terror. After a while they showed signs of confusion, and one of them broke away from the others.

This is what Dzidek has been waiting for. He dives at full speed into the breach. Before the German has time to rejoin his formation, Dzidek catches him on the beam with two short bursts. The German turns sharply and dives. Dzidek

2

THE BATTLE OF BRITAIN, 1940

ALL OF us have known those days, all lived through them, and yet we find it difficult to realize how terrible was the summer of 1940. It was a ghastly time for all men of good will. They could hardly bear the song of birds, and they had no pleasure in the warm July sunshine, or the homely delight of sharing daily bread with their nearest.

That part of humanity still unenslaved lived through days of terror. They rubbed their eyes to dispel a nightmare, only to wake to a reality even more sinister. The world was being shaken to its foundations, and dark forebodings, anxiety, fear and despair filled millions of hearts. Everybody was losing hope. Not only the sensitive, but even the most sluggish. The Thames-side cockney, the *caboclo* of Brazil, the miner of Pennsylvania, the Australian farmer and the planter of Java—all felt the same gnawing pang of uncertainty. They lived in expectation of the final defeat, not only of Britain, but of the whole civilized world. And their dread was not the result of any hostile propaganda, of Fifth Column influence, but of the cold language of fact. The logic of fact was stern and inexorable.

The facts were these: In four weeks the might of armed Germany had shattered Poland, defended by a brave and skillful army. In a few weeks it had crushed France, wealthy France, once famed for the valor of her soldiers. Five other small countries had been destroyed in passing, swiftly and brutally. The British armies had suffered two painful defeats: failure in Norway and disaster in Belgium. Fortunately they were only defeats abroad. But a great battle on British soil was in prospect, and the sequence of events which had led to it shattered confidence even in the stoutest hearts.

The situation was indeed menacing. Winston Churchill himself bluntly said so to the nation. He spoke with stern frankness about the possibility of an invasion, and declared that Britain would

THE BATTLE OF BRITAIN, 1940

fight, if necessary, in every street and every house.

The German preparations lasted six weeks from the time of the collapse of France. Their offensive began on August 8th, 1940. It was to be—as the Germans boasted—the last act of the war drama, concluding in the autumn with the British Empire shattered into the dust.

No new weapon was devised by the Germans. They used their well-tried air arm. Bombs were to decide the Battle of Britain. From August 8th onward swarms of war machines swept over England. On that first day there were three hundred, a few days later six hundred of them. The Battle of Britain had begun. It was one of the most remarkable as well as one of the most vital battles in the history of mankind. Remarkable, for it was fought entirely in the air, between a few hundred British fighters and thousands of enemy aircraft. Vital, for the fate of our civilization hung in the balance.

If the Germans had achieved air mastery over Britain the country would have been at their mercy, and the destruction of all its strategic and industrial centers would have been merely a matter of time and bomb tonnage. Defense against the actual invasion would soon have become impossible. But air mastery was the pre-requisite, and during the two months of the Battle the Germans launched ninety-eight main attacks to achieve it, using in all some 6000 aeroplanes.

Wave after wave came over with unabated violence. Aerial hordes rushed from the south and the east. Repulsed, they returned; routed, they still returned, like the many heads of an apocalyptic monster, borne on wings blazoned with the black cross.

The German pressure reached its climax by the middle of the month. General invasion was planned to begin between the 15th and 20th of September, and the German bombers were ordered to let hell loose and spread terror over the land.

On September 15th two main attacks were launched against England. They were to decide the issue. Each attacking force consisted of over 250 bombers and fighters, with an aggregate of 400,000 horse power and a corresponding capacity for destruction. England was defended by some 250 fighters, with the fire power of two thousand machine-guns. They won. 185 German aircraft

—over a third of the total—crashed in the fields of Surrey and Kent, as many again were badly mauled and barely able to reach their bases, while the rest sought safety in their speed.

The German air armada suffered an ignominious defeat: there was no invasion.

The victory in the Battle of Britain not only saved the Empire from destruction, but also freed the world from an evil obsession. It proved that the Germans can be defeated, that their arms, though deadly, are not infallible. In July 1940 the *Luftwaffe* was still undefeated. The shadow of its wings hung over the world and haunted every mind. Two months later the spell was broken; the sun shone brightly once more, and the daily bread of millions tasted good again.

All this was due to a handful of fighter pilots, young, undaunted, and brave. They were modest, smiling, strong, healthy boys. The Germans threw into battle their best machines and finest pilots, but the Hurricanes and Spitfires proved better than the enemy's best, and the R.A.F. pilots surpassed the German aces.

The Prime Minister rendered supreme tribute to the fighter pilots immediately after the first phase of the Battle. He summed up the situation admirably in the memorable words:

"Never in the field of human conflict was so much owed by so many to so few."

They were few indeed, but their victory was equal in importance to that won on the Marne in the last Great War.

Polish fighter pilots had the honor of taking part in the Battle, side by side with their British comrades. Their squadron, the famous "303" entered the Battle in its last, decisive stage and fought for 43 days—from August 30th to October 11th. Squadron 303, known also as the Kosciuszko Squadron, was carrying on the splendid tradition of the squadron formed in 1919 by a group of gallant Americans who hastened to the help of Poland. In 1940, faithful to the Kosciuszko ideal, its pilots astounded the world by their valor, and defended Britain as though it were their own land.

The Squadron's bag in the Battle of Britain 1940 was 126 German machines, 93 of them being accounted for by the Poles, 16 by the three British members, and 17 by the Czech member of the

THE BATTLE OF BRITAIN, 1940

squadron. Squadron 303 took part in a score of major encounters, and in some cases clearly decided their issue.

In the critical month of September, Squadron 303 brought down 109 German aircraft, that is 11% of the total of 964 brought down by the whole R.A.F. It had the largest number of successes of any fighter squadron in the R.A.F., while the next best squadron had 48 victories, less than half the number scored by Squadron 303.

The Squadron paid for this achievement with the lives of five of its members—a remarkably low figure, 70% below the average rate of casualties in the R.A.F. during the same month.

The day of September 15th will for ever be the day of the British fighter pilots. But it will also be memorable in the annals of the Polish pilots, and that joint anniversary is likely to remain a permanent link between the British and Polish airmen, who found a brotherhood of arms in their common victory of September 1940.

3

COMRADESHIP

Dover, the bridgehead of Great Britain, is a point of far-reaching significance. Here both land and air are important. The swollen barrage balloons hang in the sky like a flock of grazing sheep. Ridiculous and helpless, yet menacing and evil: if a daredevil of the air gets entangled in the cables he crashes to his death. To their own people they are innocent toys; to the enemy, a thorn in the flesh. So the Germans hate those balloons and obstinately attack them.

An entire squadron of Messerschmitts was coming from the south-west, the Hastings direction. Taking cover in the scattered clouds, as stealthily as thieves, the sections came along the coast to Dover. They were trying to take the town by surprise. But before they could think of diving on

COMRADESHIP

the balloons, they were themselves taken by surprise: in front the Germans descried British fighters. They were the fighters of Squadron 303.

Dover had seen no better air circus than the general dog-fight which displayed a score of machines circling, diving, turning, looping and using every aerobatic device. There was such beauty in that mad dance of planes that from the ground it seemed like a gigantic ballet, or a display of grand pageantry, rather than an episode of modern total war.

The Germans did not hold out long. Although none of them was shot, it was clear that the nimbler Hurricanes were rapidly getting on top, and frequently sat on the tails of the Messerschmitts. The enemy found the combat too hot, and quietly, one after another, left the mêlée, heading for the French coast. The sky gradually emptied over the cliffs of England, and soon only a fantastically intertwined mass of white trails was left as a souvenir of the battle. The pursuit had sped out over the Channel. The Messerschmitts fled like startled deer, furiously hunted by the Hurricanes.

The task of Squadron 303—chasing the Germans from Dover—was accomplished.

Pilot Officer Ox was among the pursuers. Two days before he had won an easy and brilliant victory, which cheered him up and made him determined to get another "Little Adolf." The Messerschmitt on which his choice had fallen seemed to anticipate its fate. It was twisting and zigzagging quite unnecessarily; obviously the pilot was losing grip of his nerves. This enabled Ox to draw nearer, flying straight at full throttle. He punched him with the first burst at a range of three hundred yards.

The German's reaction was unexpected, and Ox was dumbfounded. The Messerschmitt simply banked and went through an exhibition roll, afterwards continuing on a straight course. A silly, theatrical maneuver of no use whatever.

"A greenhorn!" thought Ox, and decided to finish him off as quickly as possible.

It was about time, too. The French coast, bristling with flak, was already well in sight.

Because of the roll the Messerschmitt had lost another hundred yards in the race. Ox took a view of him through his gun sight, and he liked what he saw: in the middle of the red ring the huge

The victors return

Scoreboard

fuselage hung like a wild gray dove, and as helpless as a dove.

His second burst streamed into the enemy machine. The Messerschmitt dived steeply. Ox went after him. But suddenly, to the Pole's horror, something dreadful happened. Everything went dark; the cockpit was covered with a mysterious curtain. A dark fluid spread over the transparent windscreen. By its greenish color Ox knew it was oil. His hair stood on end: the oil pipes must have burst.

He must at once give up the chase. He pulled out of the dive and turned back towards England. He could not finish off the German; it was now a matter of saving his own life. He opened the cockpit and tried to wipe the windscreen with his handkerchief. It helped a little.

Then a further shock. Black smoke began to pour from the exhaust. The Hurricane might catch fire at any moment. Ox loosened his straps in case he had to bale out. He waited and gazed anxiously down at the sea, which seemed like a leaden plate. No pilot likes the sea, but now it looked to Ox like the jaws of hell.

The machine did not catch fire, but something almost as serious did happen. Starved of oil, the engine began to vibrate violently, shaking the machine as though it were riding over cobbles. The pistons were seizing. Ox hurriedly turned off the petrol, and the engine stopped. He went into a glide, wondering how far it would carry him. It was his only chance.

His altitude was 20,000 feet and the English coast was about fifteen miles away. Would he get there? The plane was now only a mass of heavy metal, slowly falling out of the sky, impotent, obedient to only one will: the law of gravitation. Could he glide all that distance?

Yet that was not his only worry. There was another, much worse. Ox was frightened, for he was defenseless. It was September 2nd and the Battle was raging over England. Scores of Messerschmitts would be returning to France along this route. His crawling Hurricane, incapable of maneuvering, and trailing smoke, was visible for a radius of several miles and could be shot down easily by the clumsiest of beginners.

Ox was depressed. He felt like a man with broken arms and legs. He was no longer a proud

COMRADESHIP

fighter ready to challenge all the world to battle. He was a worm on which anyone could tread. He was a soldier without arms.

Now they had found him! Through the grimy glass he saw an airplane approaching from one side. It was five hundred yards away, now it was three hundred yards, now it should be opening fire. But for some reason it did not. Ox strained his eyes in that direction as though he could drive it off by glaring at it. But the other man did not fire. He was a friend, Pilot Officer Tolo. He had seen the Hurricane in difficulties and had come to help. He recognized Ox. With a gesture he indicated that he would remain close by and guard him.

Soon they were joined by a second Hurricane, also from Squadron 303, Pilot Officer Paszko. When Paszko saw the queer behavior of the other two he stopped pursuing the enemy and lent a hand with guarding Ox.

They covered him. They knew they were laying themselves open to the greatest danger if a more numerous enemy should attack them, for they would not flee. In defense of their comrade they were ready to perish and had not the least doubt about it: they would remain with him. Down below, in the misty uncertainties of earth the problems of life and death are a complex, tormenting, frequently insoluble enigma. At the height of 20,000 feet the problems of life, death and duty are simple and clearly defined: just as the sunlight is brighter here than at ground level.

Ox felt relieved and his nerves relaxed. The worst was over, and he had time to look after his machine. Fortunately, the smoke had gone. The pilot concentrated all his efforts on navigating and getting the maximum lift out of his wings. The three friends were all harassed by one thought: would he be able to reach the coast of England?

They passed the middle of the Channel. The land emerged more and more clearly, though the coast approached with tormenting slowness. Ox anxiously gazed again and again at the altimeter. The needle dropped relentlessly, with inflexible, cruel patience. The soundless dial seemed to be registering a verdict: 8000 feet, 7500 . . . 7200. . . .

Then the escort pilots noticed two planes far ahead. They were flying towards them, in the direction of France, and much higher. They immediately recognized them as Messerschmitt 109's. The Germans also saw the Hurricanes. Puzzled by their slow progress and smelling easy hunting, they turned off their course and flew towards them.

Paszko and Tolo prepared for the fight. They climbed above Ox and began to circle, on guard over him.

The Messerschmitts flew round the Polish section, and began to follow it with a great advantage of height. For a while they did not seem to know what to do. Then they made another wide circle and took up a position for attack, in line with the sun.

The two Hurricanes flying incessantly over Ox did not let the enemy out of their sight. Their deliberate circles were expressive of firm determination. The ring which they traced around their friend seemed almost to be drawn with a magic incantation. The enemy began to realize that before they reached the helpless Hurricane they would have to face some nasty talons.

They hesitated. They came still nearer, to five hundred yards, but they continually delayed their attack. Watching closely, they were evidently trying to seek out a weak spot in the defense.

The seconds flowed past, as pregnant as centuries. The Germans waited rather too long. Their moment had passed: irresolution had lost them their chance.

They gave it up. Suddenly they turned and flew off towards France.

The altimeter was inexorable: 5000 feet, 4500, 4000. . . . Still four miles to go, three miles. . . . The coast is steadily approaching, steadily showing more clearly. 3500 feet, 3000. . . . A thrilling race between two rivals: distance and height. Which will win? The sea is rising higher and higher; now Ox can distinguish the waves, but he can also see the little houses on the coast. Only a few more minutes, and it looks as though the wings are going to win. Yes, the wings are winning, those good, sturdy wings, faithful to their master.

The plane crosses the line of the coast, 900 feet up.

Ox had won. A human life was saved. The pilots sighed with relief and a burning feeling of gratitude filled their hearts. They had to break their silence. All official regulations went by the board.

"Hallo, hallo!" Ox called rather hoarsely into his

microphone, and when his friends replied, he said in an agitated voice:

"Thank you. . . ."

But the others took refuge in jests and laughter. Pilot Officer Tolo answered:

"Cut it out! How about some whisky?"

"I'll make it a couple!"

"Not enough! I want three!"

And while they were chaffing over the whisky, Ox looked for a field where he could make a forced landing.

High above, in the air, questions of life, death and duty find a simple and expressive formula. Three steely, inflexible powers; yet sometimes out of them springs a tender, precious flower: comradeship. A flower precious and strange, for once it has sprung up, it can withstand the keenest winds and endure the most violent of storms.

4

THE FIGHTER PILOT

He is the knightly member of the great family of the air. His task is defense—defense of his own bombers or of his own cities against enemy bombs. Sometimes he attacks the enemy on the ground, but most of his battles are fought high in the sky above the clouds, where the view is spacious, heaven is near and the ground remote. It is a world which has little in common with the earth as we know it.

The fighter pilot defends, but his defense is not of the passive Maginot type. He defends by charging at the enemy with all the thousand horsepower throbbing in his engine. The fighter always thrusts forward, always attacks by storm. All his battles are like bayonet charges.

That herd of a thousand wild, furious horses carries him along at the tremendous speed of 500 feet per second. Men walking on land cannot imagine what such a velocity means and what changes it effects in human nature. A fighter pilot —a man like all of us, when on the ground—in the air becomes a demon of speed, a living streak of lightning.

He has lived perhaps twenty-five years on the earth, and has taken several years to learn to resolve all things in a few seconds in the air. Death flies as fast as the enemy machine, and only lightning decision can check its course. Split seconds mean everything. Rescue delayed by moments may involve defeat. The great aerial battles of September 1940, frequently fought over several counties, never lasted more than ten to fifteen minutes. During those fifteen minutes the issue of the war and the fate of the Empire were at stake.

On the ground a fighter pilot lives like other men, loves, drinks and laughs. Like others, he knows why he is fighting and why he must be relentless in the fight. But on taking-off he sheds all earthly feelings: the involved complexes of hate and love are left below. In the air there is only the simplest instinct of life and the sense of playing a great game. All existence finds expression on the many dials in the cockpit, and the only object in life is to shoot down the enemy plane. During the actual fight reactions follow one another so quickly that the pilot is unable to recall their sequence, and afterwards he is left with the feeling of a mental void, a black-out. The fighter pilot who thinks of the Germans' cruelty to the Poles as he takes aim at a Dornier is just a fairy-tale hero, born in the imagination of those who walk the earth. The pilot does think of the wrongs he and his have suffered, but only before or after the fight.

In the air a fantastic biological process takes place, such as might have been dreamed of by Leonardo da Vinci, who knew that the air is rightly an element to be conquered by the human race. The belts with which the pilot is strapped to his seat have a symbolical meaning, apart from their immediate purpose. The pilot cannot move in the small cabin, which fits around him like the skull around the brain. And he is the brain of the metal bird.

A miraculous change is wrought as the machine climbs up into the sky. The man is fused with the

THE FIGHTER PILOT

mechanism, and soon they are one. The result is a new creature, half human, half superhuman. Sensitive pilots have the feeling that their sensory nerves extend to the tips of the wings. They feel those wings as physically as their own limbs, and when bullets hit a wing they have the sensation of being wounded in their own body. The engine becomes the pilot's powerful heart, and when its throb weakens death is near.

In the air sight is much the most important sense. Spotting the enemy, making a swift decision and finding the target—all depend on perfect vision. Many fighter pilots have experienced the sensation of having their eyes grow larger and larger, so that finally they seem to fill their body, which is then the machine's great eye. It needs to be large in order to serve not only the small human body, but the whole fighter creature, with its wingspan and fantastic power of speed and climb.

The complete fusion of man and machine is most obvious at the moment of firing. That is the culminating point of the fighter's whole existence —it is his life task. Almost all pilots agree that not only the sighting eye and the finger pressing the button, but all the rest of the body takes part in the act of firing. All parts of the body guiding the machine are also aiming and firing. Firing is not a separate act, but part of the co-ordinated operation of the whole human flying machine.

The bullets streaming visibly out of the wings are the fangs and claws of the beast mauling the prey. They are the living expression of the will to conquer. The tension is often so great that the pilot feels that the bullets are his arms reaching out for the enemy and rending him to pieces in the air.

The remarkable victories of the Polish fighter pilots in September 1940 were a revelation to the world, and many people sought to discover their secret. There are several reasons for their efficiency, but three seem to be the most important: superior eyesight, superior tactics, and greater resolution in attack.

Many Poles seem to be endowed with particularly keen eyes, which can spot an aeroplane at an amazing distance.

The Polish fighter pilots avoid all protracted maneuvering for position. They like to go for the enemy at the first possible moment, to close in almost to hand grips, and to open a murderous fire from their eight machine-guns at a range of less than a hundred yards. At first this method was criticized by experts, who described it as an unnecessary display of mad recklessness, but it was soon found that the "wild lads" not only had more victories to their credit, but—strangely enough—had a much lower rate of casualties than other pilots.

Every Pole has the qualities of a lancer, with a lancer's temperament and dash. Evidently this traditional characteristic is of great value four miles up, where the Polish fighter pilots carry out lancer charges, riding not one but a thousand horses. The break-up, by only five fighters, of a German bomber armada on September 15th 1940 was as gallant a deed as the famous charge of Light Horse at Somosierra, but it had a more profound moral result and brought the Poles greater glory than the Spanish adventure of 1809.

The third reason for the achievements of the Polish fighter pilots is the intensity of their determination. But if you wish to understand the savage determination of the Polish airmen, you must read another story, the story of Poland's martyrdom since September 1939.

5

ALL BULLETS SPENT

Tenacity is as deadly a weapon as a gun. The more tenacious fighter always wins. His will is stronger, his stamina superior, his eye keener, and so his bullets more often find their target.

Sergeant Kar looks a boy, only about twenty, but he is slightly older. He has a round face, quick to break into a smile, but bold, black, passionate, aggressive eyes.

One day he was with Squadron 303, chasing a German bomber formation over the Thames estuary. Others caught up with the enemy, but he did not, for a dozen German fighters attacked his section. Kar dodged them with a dive, but in doing so he lost contact with the rest of his squadron.

ALL BULLETS SPENT

Diving down, he encountered a lone Messerschmitt. He fired at once, but missed. A regular duel began, with circling, quick turns and maneuvering for position. The Hurricane finally got on to the tail of his opponent, and Kar let him have a long burst. The Messerschmitt went down, with smoke pouring from the engine.

The young pilot had carried on the dog-fight almost mechanically, with little thought and less emotion. He worked not like a man of flesh and blood, but like a machine of steel. A good piece of mechanism, developed in the old school of the Polish Air Force.

His nerves and his human passion were not aroused until a moment later. He was still watching with satisfaction the enemy's agony—the finest of sights to a fighter pilot—when a stream of tracer bullets flashed by, like a bolt out of the blue. The unexpected attack interrupted his calm contemplation of victory, and although he managed to avoid the danger with a sudden twist, he shook with dismay and anger.

"Blast you!" he swore furiously, as the Messerschmitt streaked down past him. It was followed at some distance by two Hurricanes. Without stopping to reflect, the sergeant joined in the chase.

They went down almost to water level; the German first, followed by the two Hurricanes, and then by Kar. They passed the white houses of Gravesend, bleached by sea wind and rain, and flew low, like great gulls, past the real gulls, past green meadows and gray sails—hundreds of sails and fishermen's boats.

They were flying over one of the most characteristic corners of England: the mouth of the Thames. The haze of London gave a rosy and yellow tinge to the afternoon sunlight, and here, where land and water met, it caused a strange play of light. It was a delicate picture of exquisite coloring. The magic of these lights and the exuberant beauty of the ships has attracted British painters for generations. They regard this spot as their sanctuary. The great Turner found inspiration for his paintings in these parts.

Today the roar of four engines, like hell's thunder, rent the peace of the river and deafened everything that lived over the water. It was a poignant symbol of the present, and one of unusual eloquence: a German, two Britons, and a Pole were in the flight. These four machines violating the age-old spirit of the Thames were only a tiny part of the ghastly machine; a machine that was shaking the whole world and involving all the nations. Yet its significance was summarized in the one, apparently very simple question: whether the light and the mist at the mouth of the Thames was to remain an inspiration to British genius. . . .

The Messerschmitt turned right, cutting across Kent along the shortest route to France. Kar did not like the way things were going. The German had a fine turn of speed and he might easily escape. The two Hurricanes in front were barely keeping up with him.

Kar put on full boost. The fighter screamed as though lashed by a whip, and sprang forward. Kar felt all the joy of a rider spurring a horse into a gallop. He hummed the old cavalry song:

> "Oh, it's fine when the uhlan
> Rides to war. . . ."

Racing at top speed he passed the two other Hurricanes. Near Rochester he began to overtake the Messerschmitt, now only about five hundred yards ahead. They were still flying very low. The enemy plane grew larger with every second. Kar suddenly felt a soldier's solicitude for his mount. A miraculous, a terrific machine! Going like hell!

Now he was only three hundred yards behind. With a swift glance Kar once more assured himself that his machine-gun mechanism was in order. The safety-catch was off. Without pressing the button he passed his thumb over it gently, caressingly. Yet that thumb was also like the claw of a rapacious animal. He was almost in a position to fire: the German was flying straight, and was an easy mark. . . . But it did not yet occur to Kar to fire. Closer! He must get closer! He had plenty of time. . . . The Jerry would not get away! . . .

Now only 150 yards, 100 yards, 70. . . . Good! He took aim and fired. Dead in line from the rear, right through the Messerschmitt's tail. . . . Hell! Without result! The German was still flying as though nothing had happened.

Kar, hot on the track, swung off slightly to the side and gave the enemy a second burst at an angle into his side, where it was most susceptible to attack. And this time with effect! He must have hit some vital spot. A thin streak of smoke came from the Messerschmitt, like a thin streak of blood from a wounded animal.

No, it was not a vital spot. The Messerschmitt did not burst into flame, and the smoke gradually grew thinner and thinner. The machine tore on with undiminished speed.

Kar ground his teeth. He drew still closer to the enemy; now he was right on his heels. He took aim . . . and next moment avoided a crash by only a hair's breadth.

His eyes fixed on the sight, he did not see that the Messerschmitt was flying straight at a tree. At the last moment the German pulled himself up over the treetop, while Kar all but flew straight into the tree. He pulled his machine up violently. The topmost branches struck against the bottom of the fuselage, but fortunately did no damage. The Hurricane flew on unharmed. But Kar burst into a sweat.

"Curse the blighter!" he swore at the cunning enemy.

From a merciless distance, hardly fifty yards behind the Messerschmitt, he opened fire a third time. But to his surprise and disappointment, almost to the point of pain, only a few bullets came from the guns, and then they were gloomily silent. All his ammunition was gone. And the German was still flying on. Rotten luck! though Kar at once realized that it was not surprising. It was his second adversary that day.

He turned aside to let the other two Hurricanes finish the job. But a glance back was enough to show him that they would never catch up. Too far behind.

Below them was a country town. The gray walls of a large church: possibly Canterbury Cathedral. Yes, it was Canterbury. Barely three or four minutes now to the sea. And the German was still going at full speed. Nothing could stop him, no opposition lay in his way.

Kar was seized with despair and sudden, uncontrollable hatred. His eyes glared—evil, cruel, delirious eyes. He had accounts to settle with the enemy, and not merely those of a soldier. Other, worse, human accounts! He must destroy the German at any cost. At any cost!

He went flat out again. He swung out still farther to one side, and overtook the fleeing plane.

Then, in a sudden foolhardy rush, he turned and flew—a frenzied torpedo of madness—straight at the Messerschmitt as though to crash into it.

He did not crash. He flew right above the enemy's machine; only a yard, or perhaps even less, above his glass-enclosed cockpit. For the fraction of a second Kar saw below him the German's face, upturned, frightfully distorted with mortal terror: then it passed.

Behind Kar sounded a muffled, mighty crash.

The German had failed to stand the strain. His nerve had given way. His hand trembled on the controls; one tremor was sufficient.

Gaining height, Kar turned and went back to the spot where the Messerschmitt had hit the ground. A great cloud of dust and smoke. Amid the scattered fragments tongues of flames were starting up. One wing had traveled fifty yards; the remnants of the other lay a hundred yards from the crash. Of the enemy nothing remained but a heap of rubbish.

Kar circled around and drank his fill of the scene of destruction. His eyes again had their normal look—bold, fervent, aggressive. He—a little Polish sergeant—had also drawn inspiration from the misty estuary of the Thames, his own, warlike inspiration. . . .

In this war there are no more tenacious pilots than the Poles. Their comprehensible animosity against the Germans has given rise to many stories, current all over the world, in which a dare-devil flyer, after using up his ammunition, has rammed the enemy and paid for his victory with his own life.

Truth is stranger and more beautiful than fiction: in this instance the Polish fighter pilot, with all his bullets spent, hurled himself at the enemy, but the foe was the one who crashed.

6

UPS AND DOWNS

The battle of Britain is on. Day after day German bombers invade the sky of England. They batter away at the British bastion, attempting to smash and crush it. The Germans are amazed: the bastion continues to hold out. The Germans are furious: the bastion continues to resist.

In the third week of the Battle the invaders realized that they were not yet masters of the air over England. So changing their tactics they launched the entire destructive power of the *Luftwaffe* against the British fighters and their stations. For two long weeks—at the end of August and beginning of September—the German fighters raged against the R.A.F. stations, striving to blast their British rivals out of the sky.

They had already told the world of their victory; they had announced that England was crushed, that her resistance was already broken. But every day new British squadrons, unvanquished, unbroken, audacious, started up from the ground to meet the German attack, resisting the enemy's blows, and inflicting casualties three times as large as their own. They waged an obstinate and superhuman struggle against brute force, and every day the successive waves were shattered against the hard British granite. The Germans had never expected to find it so hard.

During that period the 303 Squadron won a notable victory. Of the total of thirty-nine German planes brought down on September 5th it accounted for eight, losing only one machine, the pilot of which was wounded.

The following day, September 6th, was obviously scheduled in German plans to become the Day of Judgment for the British fighter force. The enemy came over in larger numbers than ever, and they used a new trick, extremely dangerous for the defenders. Their fighters not only escorted the bombers, but also independently patrolled the whole sky in small groups, forming a bridge reaching from the Channel deep into the country.

"The sky looked like an aquarium with lots of small fish!" said one of the pilots who fought on that day.

Nine Hurricanes from Squadron 303 took off at 8.45 A.M. Soon after, they were directed over the radio-telephone to fly south-east. Halfway between London and the coast they were disturbed to see innumerable Messerschmitt patrols, flying very high in pairs at an altitude unattainable by the Hurricanes. Some of the Germans were circling over one spot, others swept in great spirals northward. Flying too high to be seen from the ground, they only betrayed their presence by the white trails of vapor which they left behind. The crystalline sky was more and more patterned with these trails, until at last it looked as though some sinister, invisible spider were weaving a gigantic web over the country. And indeed it was a deadly spider which was preparing its web.

Despite the threat from the superior numbers of enemy fighters the Squadron continued its flight in the appointed direction. All were tensely vigilant, watching the sky above and behind them. They were flying in very unfavorable conditions, with the sun right in their eyes. It was difficult to see anything ahead. In front was spread a milky, hazy glare, a dazzling flicker of light, a curtain of mystery and unpleasant surprises.

Unexpectedly a formation of German bombers burst out of the glare. They were making in the direction of London, and passed the Squadron at some 2000 yards to the right. Behind them was a screen of Messerschmitts, which were just being engaged by a Spitfire squadron. A magnificent chance for "303"! Without hesitation the Squadron leader decided to attack and, sweeping round to the right, tore flat out towards the bombers, with his sections behind him.

They did not get far.

A horde fell on them. Like frenzied hounds, the Messerschmitts came upon them from behind, from in front, from the sides. With a triple advantage of height, speed and sun, and yet a fourth, of overwhelming numbers, they attacked the nine fighter planes. The attack was crushing. At the first round of fire Squadron Leader Krol's machine was hit. Krol, one of the finest of the Polish fighter pilots, was badly burned, and had to bale out.

A fighter pilot's skill is displayed in defense as much as in attack. While every soldier can take cover, at 20,000 feet the fighter pilot has nothing but empty air around him, and only lightning maneuver, coupled with superhuman mental control and instantaneous reaction can save him.

The sudden attack of a swarm of Messerschmitts in such favorable conditions should have wiped out the nine pilots at the first blow: it only destroyed one of them. The others juggled their way out of the ambush, and in a moment the enemy had lost their advantage of surprise. The German guns fired into the void. The battle flared up in a number of individual duels. A pandemonium of air combat. Squadron 303 bared its fangs and unsheathed its claws. It was not going to be disposed of quite so easily as that!

Seeing a yellow nose heading straight for him, Flight Officer Witur instinctively pulled hard on the stick, and his machine swung round so violently that everything went black before his eyes. He painfully realized that at this moment of weakness his enemy would shoot him down. But the German did not. On recovering his sight, Witur saw the Messerschmitt diving down in front of him. He flung himself after the German. They circled around each other once, and then again. More closely, more avidly. In the third round Witur got on to his enemy's tail and fired at a distance of sixty yards: the first Messerschmitt went out of the battle in flames.

Sergeant Kar, the little, tenacious Kar, was just finishing off a second Messerschmitt when he saw below him three Heinkel 111 bombers. He dived straight on to them and sent the right-hand Heinkel down in flames, but at the same moment he was hit by a cannon shell from a Messerschmitt. Wounded in thigh and calf, with smashed instruments, a gaping hole in his cockpit and a damaged wing, he managed to land somewhere in the south of Kent. He had given them their money's worth before going out.

Sergeant Zycz rushed to the rescue of a Spitfire which was flying straight on, apparently not knowing that a Messerschmitt was on his tail pumping bullets into him as though on a practice shoot. Zycz got the German, who after a desperate turn

UPS AND DOWNS

went down in smoke. Yet the sergeant was a second too late: the Spitfire was also hit and dived out of control, while the pilot baled out.

Meantime more Messerschmitts were flying up from all over the sky, like a pack of jackals sniffing their prey. They all headed straight for the mêlée. In the end there were over a hundred of them—so many that they got in one another's way. The Hurricanes and Spitfires still left in the battle could no longer engage in normal fight, but were forced into purely defensive maneuvers. They performed miracles of agility and skill; nevertheless they escaped from one German only to be intercepted by another. But even then they did not lose heart.

Pilot Officer Ox, himself pursued by a couple of Germans, suddenly saw a Messerschmitt in his gunsight. A long burst: the black crosses caught fire. In the ensuing confusion Ox dropped like a stone and got away. Flight-Lieut. F. also shot down a Messerschmitt, but was himself hit and had to bale out.

The battle passed its climax, and the drama was ending. The last surviving Hurricanes and Spitfires broke out of the trap. Only Messerschmitts were left, but exhausted by the combat, they turned back towards France, on their last gallons of fuel. Space grew empty and the roar died away. Silence again descended over the Kentish Weald and valleys. On the ground the wrecks of airplanes were burning out. A few parachutes, like full-blown blossoms, were still dropping from the sky.

That day Squadron 303 suffered heavy casualties: out of nine machines five were destroyed, and four pilots were wounded. No lives were lost. But the Squadron accounted for seven German machines. Yet the true significance of the victory is not to be sought in the ratio of Polish to German losses. It is rather in the fact that on the day the Germans intended to strike the final blow against the British Fighter force, Squadron 303, by its determined attack and furious resistance, drew the greater part of the German blow down on itself, and dissipated its power. Squadron 303, together with one squadron of British Spitfires, played the part of an aerial *Winkelried*, drawing the full force of the attack upon itself, and so saving others. The German plans were once more foiled.

The formation of enemy bombers which escaped from right under the Squadron's noses flew on with a weaker air escort. It did not reach its objective. In more distant parts of England, Fighter Command threw further squadrons into the attack upon the Germans, and easily shattered them.

At last the parachutists landed. No sign of the battle was left in the heavens, except the white trails of vapor, and these also slowly melted away in the azure. The spider-web fell impotently apart. The symbol of the menacing spider vanished.

Over England the sky was again clean. . . .

The same day Squadron 303 received the following letter from the Commander-in-Chief of the Polish Armed Forces:

London, 6th September 1940.

"I congratulate Squadron 303 on its splendid day's fighting."—This message has been sent to me by the Air Minister, Sir Archibald Sinclair. After the words of H.M. King George VI in his answer to the President of Poland, this is the second message of appreciation for the valor of the Polish airmen. Fighting for some days side by side with their famous British colleagues, they have already achieved important successes. Their deeds are the only worthy reply that a Pole can give to the infamous lies of German propaganda.

SIKORSKI
C. in C.

Uhlan rides to war

. . . modest, smiling

7

BIG GAME: DORNIERS

SEPTEMBER 7th was warm and sunny. It had been quiet all day. Only at 4.32 P.M. did the blow fall: then the Germans got through to London.

As usual the city was enjoying the blessed peace of the week-end. It was Saturday. In the East End the working people were taking things easy in their back streets: the children were playing in the roads, thousands of men and women were at football matches and dog races.

At 4.30 the first small white bouquets appeared in the south-eastern sky: the A.A. guns were putting up their shells. Further bouquets appeared closer and still closer; sirens wailed, the barrage of gunfire grew louder with the roar of dozens of machines, and suddenly a torrent of death and disaster poured down. Explosive and incendiary bombs fell like hail. On warehouses, on the people's homes, on women and children, petrol tanks, gardens, docks, racecourses, gasworks, they rained down continually, as though intended to wipe the East End of London from the face of the earth.

Tanks burst, docks flamed to the skies, warehouses burned, people perished.

Without doubt the German airmen enjoyed the spectacle of this hell, laughing a devilish laugh. They were delighted beyond measure that at last, in broad daylight, they had been able to inflict bloody wounds in the very heart of the hated Empire. They were puffed up, too, with the certainty of victory, because the British Fighter Force no longer existed. For surely, if it still existed, would it have let them through to London so easily?

And in fact, the German bombers—there were about forty of them—were flying in close formation, while above them were as many Messerschmitts acting as a screen. There is no point in denying it: that was a black day for London and a black day for the Fighter Command.

Squadron 303 was sent up late—only a few minutes before the bombs began to fall on the city—and was immediately ordered to the north of

London. Then, on a south-easterly course, it was directed towards the London docks. In the distance they could see the smoke of artillery fire, and a moment later they descried the German bomber formation to the right, ahead of them. The bombers were flying much lower than the Squadron, but the Messerschmitt escort was much higher. The bombers, approaching the Thames from the south, dropped bombs on its banks, then flew northward, across the river.

The pilots thought that Flight-Lieut. F., commanding the Squadron that day, would at once turn them towards the enemy and by a sudden attack prevent the bombing of the docks if at all possible. But nothing like that happened. Apparently he did not realize the direction of the enemy's flight, and so continued to lead the fighters on the same course. The Squadron passed the Germans some two thousand yards ahead of them, and began to increase the distance between it and them. It was a critical moment. A few more seconds along the same course and the Squadron would have irrevocably lost the chance of attacking.

In the circumstances Flight Officer Paszko, who

led the second section, decided to take the initiative. He was a fighter pilot of long experience and had shown himself a model flyer and also an energetic soldier. Dipping his wings as a signal to the following machines, he broke formation with his section, turned right and simultaneously dived. The German bombers were some hundreds of yards below and now almost in the rear of the Squadron. Flying Officer Dzidek and Flight Lieut. Witur, leading the third and fourth sections, followed him, also turning sharply. Fortunately the first section, led by F., quickly noticed their colleagues' maneuver and turned back, now occupying the rear position.

While the Squadron was thus swinging round in a great arc, high above it an action of great importance and advantage to the "303" fighters was just developing. A few seconds earlier a second squadron of Hurricanes had appeared out of the blue and had vigorously attacked the bombers' fighters screen. In consequence the majority of the Messerschmitts were engaged and the bombers were deprived of effective protection.

The bombers were Dornier 215's. Flying in sections of three, they kept in close formation, so creating a solid, mutually defensive force. In theory this flying fortress had a tremendous firing power of more than 120 machine-guns. But a single fighter squadron, every member a daredevil of aerial acrobatics and deadly in attack, had this mass of bombers as impotent and defenseless as a tortoise turned on to its back.

The slaughter that followed was terrible. It was a massacre such as rarely occurs in air warfare. Paszko's section was the first to attack, falling on the tail of the bomber formation. Witur's section tore into the right flank, Dzidek's section into the left flank. F.'s section struck at the leading machines. Thus the Germans were attacked from all sides by twelve infuriated hornets with murderous stings. Or like twelve raging hounds tearing at the fat body of a boar.

They tore that body to pieces.

The first Dornier burst into flames under Paszko's fire. On the left flank Sergeant Szaposzka pulled down a second machine. Sergeant Wojt on the right flank got a third. The fourth, hit by Pilot Officer Tolo, "burst like a bubble." Pilot Officer Jan Donald dealt with the fifth. Then two fighters of the first section, the Canadian F. and the Pole Joe, simultaneously cleared out two more. Meantime Witur was setting yet another ablaze, Paszko was handling his second victim, and Wojt also had got another.

It all happened incredibly swiftly, smoothly, almost gracefully, as though on a sports field. The Dorniers fell out of the sky like partridges out of the covey, sometimes a brace at a time.

The attack had developed so rapidly that only at this stage did Messerschmitts, unengaged by the Hurricanes above, come flying down to help. They arrived too late. The bombers were shattered, routed. Those still intact tore off at full speed for France, in ones and twos, as best they could, all blinding out of it in confusion and panic. No longer were the Germans chuckling; gone were their smiles. The incendiaries of London's suburbs were themselves perishing in the flames of their own machines. The remnants fleeing over East Anglia were caught and destroyed by other Hurricanes and Spitfires.

Some pilots of Squadron 303 turned to tackle the Messerschmitts. Flying Officer Dzidek shot one down, Sergeant Szaposzka another, and Flying Officer Pis a third. Pis ran into trouble with

BIG GAME: DORNIERS

his man: his machine was shot up and he had to bale out. As he jumped his left shoe caught on the edge of the cockpit, and for some time he went on with his machine, hanging head downwards. At last he managed to wrench his foot out of his shoe and made a safe landing in his socks. He felt ashamed of himself, for his sock had a hole in it.

Pilot Officer Donald was the last to shoot up a bomber, his second. When the Dorniers were seized with panic, one of them, blind with fear, ran right across Donald's line of fire at a distance of twenty yards. After the first burst such a long tail of fire burst from it that the Pole, alarmed for his own machine, turned violently away. He lost consciousness, and recovered only when he had dropped some twelve thousand feet and found himself (only just in time) above a flaming suburb.

In this fight Squadron 303 shot down 14 German machines for certain and had four probables. Its own casualties were two machines lost, one man wounded and one shoe lost. The same day other R.A.F. squadrons shot down 61 Germans, losing 20 fighters. The anti-aircraft artillery brought down 28 raiders. It was the A.A.'s best day since the beginning of the war. . . .

Seeing new waves of German bombers approaching from the south, Flight-Lieut. Witur landed on the first R.A.F. airdrome east of London in order to get more fuel and ammunition. The airdrome seemed to be empty. He taxied across the whole field, but found no one there.

Black smoke rose from the burning suburbs of London, darkening half the sky. It looked from that particular R.A.F. station as though all London were on fire. Somewhere close by, anti-aircraft artillery was putting up a strong barrage. The distant thud of bombs indicated that the raid was not yet over.

Eventually a British corporal appeared and gave Witur a friendly invitation to come into the shelter. There the pilot found several soldiers, the crew of a machine-gun section who were guarding the station. It was just five o'clock and tea-time. The soldiers calmly drank tea—as they chatted, smoking cigarettes. They did not care a damn for what was going on outside: it was tea-time.

BIG GAME: DORNIERS

"Have a cup of tea?" asked the hospitable corporal, pouring it out without waiting for a reply.

A bomb fell nearby and shook the shelter a little.

"What ho!" laughed the corporal, and continued to spread jam over his bread.

Witur could not stand it. His nerves were still strained with the recent battle. That phlegmatic five-o'clock tea-party seemed to him a bad dream. He asked the corporal to take him at once to the ground staff. The corporal took him along to the fitters. They, too, were having tea in a shelter, but they gave him what he wanted. As he took off, Witur felt as though he were awakening from a nightmare. Back once more in his own element, he felt better; his anger passed and he smiled. But the words still kept humming in his head: "A cup of tea. . . . A cup of tea. . . ."

At 20,000 feet he came on the track of German bombers. The ground lay far below and he was his true self again. He laughed as he remembered the corporal, and suddenly he realized the profound truth about this island of Britain: such a nation must win, even though the Germans burned all London down.

8

SUFFERING

JOE, as his British friends call him, has always been rather a mystery. It is easy to mistake him for quite a different kind of man from what he actually is. Once a sailor made that mistake and tried to borrow his girl from the frail pilot, deceived by Joe's mild smile and shy look. But Joe promptly knocked him down, for he can pull a hefty punch, for all his light build, and there is plenty of fight behind his quiet and diffident appearance.

Joe's pleasant smile and his blue, untroubled eyes conceal another unexpected fact—that he has gone through the agonies of hell.

He had brought down a German bomber on the September day of the slaughter of Dorniers. Afterwards, amid the general confusion, he chased

SUFFERING

the Germans beyond Dover, but there his luck ended. Surrounded by Messerschmitts, he got a cannon shell right in his cockpit. The explosion tore out pieces of flesh from his thigh, his side and his shoulder. Half of his body was paralyzed with pain, while hot glycol from the radiator, splashing all over him, scalded his face. The cabin was filled with acrid smoke.

In spite of the shock and his wounds, Joe's mind remained clear. He had no desire whatever to perish. But how to escape? The machine was as badly damaged as Joe himself; the control cables broken, with the stick wagging limply.

His Hurricane went into a spin. Every turn mixed more blood with the oil and glycol, and clutched at the pilot's brain with a horrible grip of pain. Yet he must do something. Only a few seconds were left. The spinning machine was heading straight for the ground.

There was only one thing to be done: he must bale out. Joe opened the cockpit and tried to jump, but found he was too weak to get out. The pressure of the air pushed him back and closed the door. He struggled desperately. At last he managed by a superhuman effort to pull himself to the edge of the cockpit with his one sound hand, but then the oxygen and radio leads connected to the flying suit tied him to the doomed machine. Straining all the muscles of his lacerated body, like a beast on a chain, he succeeded in breaking the leads and jumped into the void.

Then two sensations, of surprise and fear, took possession of him. He was surprised not to have been hit by the tail of the spinning machine. And he was afraid of the Messerschmitts above. The Germans like to shoot helpless pilots as they parachute to the ground. There were many enemy planes about. So Joe preferred not to open his parachute too early.

He was dropping in a strange position: lying on his back, face upwards. He could not see the ground at all and his body was still spinning round and round. Sometimes he would see a strip of land, at the edge of the swaying sky. But that was only the horizon, and he could not tell how far he had fallen. Suddenly panic seized him. Maybe the ground was already getting near? He had lost all sense of time and altitude. Had he been falling minutes, or only fractions of a sec-

SUFFERING

ond? He tried in vain to twist his neck to see the ground. He began to count: one, two, three, but soon gave it up; his thoughts scattered like smoke —and why count, anyway? His panic grew worse; the Messerschmitts no longer existed, only the pit into which he was falling, with its bottom approaching so near! Enough! Pull the ripcord!

But the parachute must be opened with the right hand. Joe's right hand was wounded and useless. He tried with his left, but the handle seemed out of reach. Death was near, damnably near. Joe wanted to fight and to live. His left hand convulsively sought for the ripcord. Anything to live!

The sudden drop from 20,000 feet and the change of pressure were bursting his lungs. He felt his head splitting. Suddenly his hand gripped something cold. The metal handle! He tugged at it. He heard a swish behind him. The parachute was opening. He knew he was saved.

When the parachute opened it pulled him up sharply and brought him into a normal position, head upwards. The jerk racked him with new pain, so piercingly that he thought he would go mad. The parachute harness was pressing on his wounded thigh. The terrible agony grew in intensity, but there was nothing he could do to relieve it. He did not lose consciousness; on the contrary, the wind refreshed him. It was beyond endurance. He tried to loosen the straps, though that would have been suicide. Fortunately, he was too weak to succeed. So he just dropped and suffered.

The parachute had opened at about 6000 feet. Ages seemed to have passed, and the earth still seemed as far away as ever. The wind began to drive him over the sea, and there was a moment when he was actually hanging over water, but this new danger meant little to him. Later, much later, the wind shifted, and he was carried back over the land.

Finally he landed near a village. The parachute dragged him over the hard clods of plowed earth, but by now Joe was indifferent to all pain.

He heard human voices. Men were running after him. They caught him by the legs and checked his drag. That was more torture, for the parachute pulled him in one direction and the men pulled by his wounded leg in the other. Seeing his strange uniform, brought from France, and his Polish badges, they mistook him for a German, and treated him roughly.

"Not German! Polish!" protested Joe in a feeble voice, and tried to smile.

When his nationality was at last settled and the parachute mastered, there was a further difficulty in setting him free. Nobody knew how to unfasten the harness, and he could not show them. They fumbled, pulled and manipulated. Joe, quite helpless, suffered, while they struggled, until at last someone cut the ropes with a knife.

Before the ambulance arrived they bandaged his leg. All were eager and friendly, some holding him still while others tied the bandages.

A stalwart Home Guard held his right arm in an iron grip, just where it was injured. Joe begged him to take his hand off, moaned and prayed. But he had forgotten his English and kept on whispering in Polish:

"Let my arm go, friend! Let go, you devil! My arm! Oh, God!"

But all to no effect. It was not until the hefty Home Guard saw blood on his own hand, after it had soaked the sleeve, that he realized his error and loosened his grip, saying good-naturedly:

"Oh, I am so sorry!"

When Joe was put on the ambulance he fell asleep, or rather, he fainted. . . .

He left the hospital after three and a half months. He had grown thinner, but his wounds had healed. His old strength and his old fighting spirit had returned. Now Joe is chasing Dorniers and Messerschmitts again.

But the strangest and most striking thing about him are his eyes and his smile. Joe still has the sunlight in his eyes and a childlike joy in his smile. His sufferings and weeks of fever did not break him, left no evil traces on him. He retained his fundamental cheerfulness.

His invincible vitality is deeply moving, and at times, as you look at this indomitable young giant you get the impression that he is more than a brilliant fighter pilot. He is the symbol of an immortal race. For his pain and wounds, and his sunlit eyes and smile, are truly symbolic of a victorious though wounded nation.

Like a shot partridge

Like hostile arrows

9

JAN DONALD SMILES THREE TIMES

PILOT OFFICER Jan Donald was the rear guard of the section. He circled warily behind the others, watching for Messerschmitts. There were plenty of them about. Besides the enemy squadron which the Hurricanes had already engaged, he could see separate German planes all over the sky, mostly very high up, but some not more than a thousand yards away from him.

England was invisible, though they all knew that it was below the fluffy carpet of the clouds which glowed in the eerie light of September sunshine. This detachment from earth suddenly inspired Donald with the odd idea that there was no ground at all, that everything was happening in a magic dreamland—everything, even the savage dog-fight above.

"Magic!" Donald said aloud in his cockpit and smiled at himself. Yet he was a sober-minded fighter pilot and no dreamer.

He was suddenly alarmed by the strange disappearance of the plane leading the section. It had been there a few seconds ago, and Donald lost sight of it when making one of his precautionary sweeps. There were some clumps of clouds here and there, like scattered bushes in a desert. The leader must have vanished behind one of them. But now he appeared again, rather higher than before, about five hundred yards ahead. Yes, that was the section leader, Donald decided with relief.

He put on a spurt and swiftly overtook the other plane. When he was less than a hundred yards behind he reduced speed, in order to come automatically into line with the leader. Suddenly he noticed a peculiar detail about the other plane. The tailplane was supported by two struts, though no Hurricanes had any such struts. He stared in amazement—he had keen, Polish eyes—and he clearly saw those two struts. What the devil!

He was flying directly in line with this strange phenomenon, so to get a better view he swerved out. He was dumbfounded: the other machine had yellow horizontal bands and a black cross on its side. A German cross! It was a Messerschmitt!

For a moment Donald's hair stood on end, and he slumped in his seat. Then from a little above, without wasting time for correction, he pumped a heavy burst into the German. At that distance the bullets rent the fuselage like a sharp ax. Bits flew off the Messerschmitt and part of one wing fell right away. Pouring out smoke, the plane plunged down, and was nothing but a flaming torch by the time it disappeared in the clouds.

Donald watched it go with glittering eyes.

"Magic!" he whispered, just a little surprised, and smiled again—this time over his victory. . . .

He was about to renew his search for his leader, when unexpectedly another Messerschmitt, flying to his colleague's aid, fell on him from above. Donald was swinging round in a circle at that moment, and this saved him: all the enemy's bullets passed by him. He saw them streaming past.

He jumped as though scalded. He climbed to get on equal terms for a dog-fight. But the German was no fool, and would not let him get to grips. Exploiting his superior speed, he dived, but climbed up sharply and regained his advantage of height. Then he dived once more, firing as he came. So he pecked again and again, like an infuriated bird. Donald took his machine into narrower and narrower circles. That was his only hope: it is difficult to hit a plane as it is turning.

The two pilots were possessed with a wild determination. They knew it was death for one of them. The German had the advantage. He fired. Donald could not fire. He kept on the defensive. But as he circled round he slowly took his machine higher. With superhuman effort he drew nearer to the enemy. He knew he was done for if he did not get level with him and force him into equal combat.

Then, oh heck! a second Messerschmitt joined in. Immediately the two enemy machines changed their tactics. They did not attack. They flew round in circles, just like Donald, only higher, above him. It was as though they were keeping guard over him. As indeed they were.

And still no end to it! Two more Messerschmitts now! They appeared above him for a moment, then disappeared again. They must be somewhere near at hand, plotting something. Four of them! That was too much! Donald no longer thought of going in to fight. His own idea was to escape, to save his life. To flee down to the clouds. He looked down, and was aghast: below him, just above the clouds, another Messerschmitt was circling. A fifth! It was cutting off his escape.

Though Jan Donald had plenty of guts and was a fearless pilot, at that moment, surrounded and held as though in a cage, he could not suppress a feeling of fear: a cold shiver ran down his back. But he had nerves of steel, and his brain did not stop working for one moment. He abandoned the apparently attractive idea of making a mad dive into the clouds. Though they were no more than fifteen hundred feet below, he knew well enough that before he could reach them the Messerschmitts would be right on his tail and would get him with their first burst. He chose another method, though it called for extreme self-control: he would not try any sudden attempt to break out, but would go on circling round, little by little dropping down closer and closer to the clouds. He was an old hand, and had firm control of his machine and himself.

Now he saw what the second pair of Messerschmitts which had vanished were up to. They had climbed much higher, and swooped down out of the sun to attack him. First one came at him in a long power-dive, opened fire, missed, and as soon as he pulled his machine out of the dive to climb up again into the sun, the other followed him down. At last Donald understood all their devilish plan: while three Messerschmitts—two above and one below—watched his every movement, keeping him in the trap, the other two could calmly attack, passing him from one to the other until the final blow was administered.

Fortunately the second burst of fire also missed, and so did the third. Meantime Donald had dropped quite a considerable distance, and was now in dangerous proximity to the fifth Messerschmitt.

Then something unforeseen occurred which completely changed the situation. The variable fortunes of war took a new turn for the fighters.

At the fourth attack the German bullets again missed him, flying over his head, and passed close to the fifth Messerschmitt. The German pilot failed to realize where the fire was coming from, and deciding that a second Hurricane had come up to attack him, he suddenly broke away and dived down towards the clouds. Then events happened in lightning succession. Donald followed his example. He was dead in line with the Messerschmitt, less than three hundred feet above him. Instinctively he got him in his sight, and pressed the button. He had got him! The German went in a helpless glide into the clouds. Donald followed him.

He reached the clouds. He had escaped from the trap. He was safe. Numbed and shaken, but alive and whole. His instruments also seemed to have been shaken up by the struggle, for his compasses and artificial horizon were refusing to function.

When Pilot Officer Jan Donald landed at his airdrome among his friends some fifteen minutes later, he asked for a glass of water and a cigarette. His colleagues looked anxiously at his parched lips: in the corners of his mouth were flecks of blood.

But Donald smiled at his friends through the blood—a smile of relief and satisfaction.

10

THE CLOUD

THE TIMES are past when man looked up at the clouds as at something distant and unattainable; a source of anxiety to farmers and of inspiration to poets and artists. The clouds have today an altogether different importance: they belong to human life, and human life may depend on them. For the airmen, especially for the fighter pilot, the clouds are what dense forests used to be for pioneers in virgin countries: sometimes the menace of an ambush and sometimes the blessing of salvation. The background of Fenimore Cooper's romantic stories was green and grew on the ground; that of modern romance is white and billows across the sky.

Pilot Officer Jan Donald saved his life by a dash into the clouds. Strangely enough, another pilot

THE CLOUD

of Squadron 303, Sergeant Zycz, had a similar adventure at exactly the same time, about twenty miles farther west. He also had been attacked by a group of Messerschmitts, and he also had tried to dodge their bullets by sharply twisting. Before the Germans had had time to organize a proper chase, Zycz broke away from their guns and fled into the clouds.

Unfortunate he could take shelter in only a single cloud, huge, but detached from the others, like an island. It was a spherical cumulus a mile in diameter, flattened at top and bottom.

The pilot was completely hidden in the cloud. There he felt perfectly safe. It was a relief. The light gray cotton-wool around him was so thick that he could not see his own wing-tips. He flew blind, depending only on his instruments. He kept at a constant height and described circles half a mile in diameter in the middle of the cloud.

When, after circling a few times, he was able to think more coolly, he began to consider the situation. An escape from the side or the top of the cloud was impossible for he knew that the Messerschmitts were there. He could only go down, and once decided he did not hesitate. His fuel was running short; he had enough for another half hour perhaps, so he had to act quickly.

He pushed the stick forward, and knew by the increased pressure on his back that he was diving. He reached the bottom of the cloud which was somewhat denser, and the next moment brilliant daylight struck him almost like a blow. He had shot out of the cloud.

He found Messerschmitts on guard below also. There were five or six of them, and they were firing at someone in the cloud. Evidently there was another machine there. He had hardly gone a hundred yards when he saw spinning trails around his Hurricane. They were German tracer bullets aimed at him. He realized that there was no escape this way, so he pulled his machine out of the dive and zoomed up. The blood flowed away from his head, and his eyes went dark, but he held on to the stick until he was safely back in the cloud.

The friendly cloud. But its friendliness had an unpleasant aspect. The fighter pilot is like a bird: he must see far, must see where he is flying. Space is his element. But in a cloud he is sightless. That is an unbearable feeling, all the more

THE CLOUD

so when another plane is also flying blind close at hand in the same cloud. Two friends circling in the dark and threatening each other with death.

Sergeant Zycz is very young, younger than any of his friends. He had dreamed of great flights, of victorious battles, and if he ever thought about death, it was one of glory. Not like this: colliding with a friend, stupidly, uselessly. He felt like a mouse escaping from a cat's claws straight into a trap.

He made another attempt to break out. Instead of diving down he tried to slip out sideways. No luck! He nearly crashed into two Messerschmitts. A sharp turn and a dash back into the cloud before the enemy had time to fire.

The cloud had saved him again. Zycz went on flying round in circles. But time was passing too, the seconds and minutes. He had less and less fuel. And also less hope. Though shielded by the friendly cloud, he began to hate it. It was a treacherous friend. His young soldierly mind could not accept the idea of a friend who is also an enemy. Something began to give way inside him. His nerve was going. He saw the other plane rushing towards him, as seamen of old used to see the Flying Dutchman. Time and again the phantom fighter appeared in the haze before him, and vanished. Was it an illusion or a real machine? Zycz did not know, but he felt terrified.

The cloud was a friend no more; it imbued him with fear. It confused his thought. He had only one desire: to escape from this throttling blindness while there was time; to break out into open space, to see the wide sky and the vast world, the blessed world of the airmen. Otherwise he would let go the stick, and break down. He would go mad; the madness of explorers lost in the trackless jungle.

Zycz saved himself from the horror. He fled. He no longer turned, but flew straight on. He cut through the edge of the cloud and burst out into sunshine. There was nobody in front. He did not look sideways. He was blinded. He flew straight on. A flicker of hope; perhaps he would win out. . . . A sudden crack, and a terrible wave of heat from his machine. Even though he did not see the flames, he knew the engine was on fire. They had got him. They had got him after all!

Hot oil splashed over his face. He felt weak

with the heat, near to fainting, and the feeling was almost a pleasant relief. He tore off the straps fastening him in the cockpit. He still had enough presence of mind to pull up the machine and turn off the petrol. He opened the cockpit. The wind was refreshing, like cold water. One more effort, and the wind did the rest; it dragged him out of the cockpit.

Immediately on jumping Zycz did something very foolish. He opened the parachute. He should have waited, to increase his distance. The enemy was still near. But it was too late when he thought of it, for already the white dome was unfolding with a flapping sound.

That enemy knows only the law of the jungle in its most brutal form: destroy ruthlessly, even the defenseless, and especially the defenseless. Zycz, hanging impotently in his harness, looked up and saw two Messerschmitts approaching. He accepted the fact as the inevitable consequence of his blunder. He felt indifferent, as he went into a light swoon. The rarefied air at that height coming after the fire bath in the cockpit would be enough to account for it.

After two minutes he came round. He was still

falling. He was still alive. And would live. Three Spitfires had come on the scene and driven away the Messerschmitts. Now they were guarding the parachute. Sergeant Zycz dropped safely to earth and to new life.

It had been a friendly cloud. Perhaps he should have trusted it more. For in the sky the same holds true as on earth: friendship, even friendship between man and nature, must be based on the age-old law of confidence.

11

THE BEST SCORE

". . . THE NEXT seven days may decide the issue of the whole world. There never has been a more critical week in world history. The perils of any Nazi attempt to invade Britain at once are manifold. But it is now or never for them. If they flinch we win. . . ." So wrote Mr. J. L. Garvin in the *Observer* for the week which opened on September 7th, 1940, with the first ferocious German attack on London.

The second attack came the same night, and new fires broke out while the old ones were still smoldering. Thenceforth night after night hordes of roaring bombers flew over the capital under the cover of darkness. Their aim was obvious: to smash the giant city's vital arteries, to break the spirit of the nine millions of human beings and change them in to a hungry, riotous mob, thus forcing the British Government to capitulate.

Whatever visions of a ruined London the German Staff cherished, its calculations went wrong: they did not take into account the size of that huge human anthill and, as usual, they overlooked psychological factors. The death of a few hundred, and later of a few thousand civilians and the ruin of some hundreds of buildings were as nothing in that vast acreage of streets and those millions of human lives. London, enormous, well balanced and strong, with good humor but yet with mounting anger, shook off the dust every morning and went cheerfully about its business.

During that period of heavy night raids the Germans also continued their day attacks; they knew the Battle of Britain could be decided only by a daylight victory. After the harsh punishment which they had received on Saturday, September 7th, they spent the Sunday licking their wounds, and did not return to the attack until Monday. Then they came in force, but lost 52 machines without securing any result. The next day was again ominously quiet, and then came the fiery Wednesday of September 11th.

THE BEST SCORE

Over several days British reconnaissance had reported a feverish and mysterious activity on the other side of the channel. The Germans were concentrating barges and troops. It looked as though serious business was afoot. The great invasion of Britain was obviously at hand. The decisive moment was approaching.

Apparently in order to hasten that moment, on September 11th the Germans carried out a powerful air attack, one of the fiercest so far.

At about four P.M. several small formations crossed the coast at various points, for the purpose—as was soon evident—of distracting the defense. For, a few minutes later, the main enemy force arrived and made straight for London. It was an air armada composed of about sixty bombers, Heinkel 111's and Dornier 215's, escorted by about forty Messerschmitt 110's flying above, with another fifty Messerschmitt 109's still higher above and behind the main formation. The German bombers expected that their strong escort would enable them to break through to London.

Not all of them got through. In spite of their numbers and stratagems, the bombers were mauled on the way. That day Squadron 303 achieved its best score, perhaps an R.A.F. record. In less than a quarter of an hour its twelve fighters shot down seventeen German machines.

The Squadron was flying south-east, directed by instructions from the ground, when it saw the enemy bombers, already about fifteen miles inland. The Hurricanes were flying higher than the bombers, but below the Messerschmitts.

It was a very ticklish situation and there was really only one sensible thing to do: to try to engage the German escort. All the more so as a British fighter squadron had just come into sight a little lower down and was heading for the bombers, to bar their way. But Flight Lieut. F., commanding the first section and in charge of the entire squadron, decided to attack the bombers too, despite the tremendous risk of flying under 90 Messerschmitts.

When the first section, followed by the others, turned towards the bombers at full speed, the expected happened. The Messerschmitts dived to the attack. But before they had time to get at Flight Lieut. F. and his two companions, the second section, led by Flying Officer Paszka, dashed forward to intercept them. The three Poles and a number of the Germans joined in a violent, confused struggle. This helped not only the first, but also the third section, led by Flying Officer Arsen, who by-passed the dog-fight and went on unchecked to get the bombers. In the meantime other Messerschmitts dived down, but they were met by the fourth section, led by Flying Officer Dzidek.

That was one of the most moving episodes of the war: six fighter pilots, desperately struggling for their lives, doubling and re-doubling their forces, by their fierce determination held up overwhelming numbers of the enemy. By all the tokens they should have been immediately crushed and torn to pieces. But it was they who shattered the enemy, and that was the strangest feature of all. They paralyzed the Germans so effectively that they formed an impenetrable barrier, below which the six other fighters could attack the bombers from the rear. And attack they did. At the same moment the whole British squadron of twelve fighters, which had now arrived, attacked the bombers from the front.

The bomber armada, caught between two fires, could not face that. Not because they suffered heavy casualties. They lost only relatively few machines. Flight Lieut. F. at once shot down a Dornier, Sergeant Brzeza got a Heinkel, Sergeant Frantisek another Heinkel, and the British pilots attacking in front also set two or three bombers on fire. But these losses did not decide the battle. The deciding factor was the German terror. Confident in the overwhelming superiority of their escort, they had never expected such audacity. They were dumbfounded; they lost their heads. They began to unload their bombs hastily, as frightened vultures unload their stomachs. Breaking formation, the bombers scattered in a wild panic. Some turned back towards France, others went blindly on towards Ireland. And although the Messerschmitts at once came down to drive off the devilish Hurricanes—and did succeed in driving them off—no power could restrain their panic-stricken flight. The panic was general. The great German force broke up into helpless parts, like the body of a leper.

This result was achieved not only by the audacity of the eighteen Hurricanes which directly attacked the bombers, but above all by the six fighters led by Paszko and Dzidek, who for half a minute or so—seconds vital for the issue of the battle—held up and disorganized the entire German escort. Flying Officer Paszko's resolute decision to engage the Messerschmitts at the right moment and the daring with which he carried it out were like grains of sand thrown in the gears of a huge machine.

After the break-up of the formation and its consequent reduction to impotence, came the second, final stage of the battle—the pursuit and extermination of the fleeing enemy. Other British squadrons also took part in the chase, as well as the six fighters which had been fighting the German escort and had miraculously escaped unscathed from the grip of the Messerschmitts. It was a strange pursuit, for at first the Germans had superior numbers, and it was not always clear who was the hunter and who the hunted.

It was an heroic struggle, fought over several counties between London and the Channel coast. Squadron 303's fighter pilots once more proved their invincible valor, intrepid pertinacity and skill. They took toll of all the German planes that ventured over England that day: Heinkels, Dorniers, Messerschmitt 109's and 110's. Two

SQUADRON 303

pilots of "303" each shot down a German, six shot down two each, and a ninth shot down three. Sergeant Szaposzka scored a genuine double. He overtook two Messerschmitt 110's flying side by side, shot both rear gunners and then, with the same burst of fire, brought down the two machines almost simultaneously. Other British squadrons which had arrived also did well.

Two Poles lost their lives in that battle. They died like heroes. Flying Officer Arsen, leading his section against the bombers, was caught in the cross-fire of German gunners and was shot through the head. Sergeant Wojt, attacked a few minutes later by nine Messerschmitts, fought like a wildcat. Despite their superiority, the Germans could not catch him. The whole population of Biggin Hill held their breath as they watched the combat. Wojt shot down two Germans before the others riddled his Hurricane with bullets. At Biggin Hill the story of the Polish sergeant's single-handed fight and death is still told.

That day Squadron 303 shot down 17 German planes, a quarter of the total of 67 brought down by all the squadrons engaged. The Germans were not easy meat. The fighting was exceptionally

THE BEST SCORE

fierce, as is shown by the allied losses, larger than on most days: 24 machines lost and 17 pilots killed.

Such was the outcome of that day of German hopes. One of the days in "the most critical week in world history"—and a day of new glory for Squadron 303. A handful of fighter pilots, or Churchill's famous "few," gave a new turn to history. The German barges waited in vain for their orders.

And that night when under cover of darkness the German bombers again came over London, they were given a fresh surprise. They ran into the heaviest artillery barrage they had ever known. Not one bomb was dropped on London. For the first time for several nights the Capital slept in peace.

12

THE ENEMY'S DANSE MACABRE

OLD SPORTSMEN, experienced hunters who know the forest and the habits of animals, know which tracks to ambush. The Hurricane and Spitfire hunters also know well where to look for their quarry and where to get them most easily: somewhere along the Channel coast when the weary flyer is returning from a generally unsuccessful expedition. The fighter pilots of Squadron 303, after carrying out their team-work, like to fly above the the coast and lie in wait. It is a good and useful sport, and in the squadron it is called "Frantisek's method."

That is what Pilot Officer Tolo did on the great day when Squadron 303 alone shot down seventeen Germans. Tolo was one of the gallant six who had effectively engaged and held off a swarm

THE ENEMY'S DANSE MACABRE

of Messerschmitts. But in a struggle with one Messerschmitt he had a hard job. He lost contact with his squadron, and by the time he got the German he was quite near to the Channel. There was no point in returning to his formation, for it had scattered all over the sky. So he just hung about the coast, in case something turned up.

It did. After a few minutes he saw the familiar outline of a Dornier 215 coming from inland. The German was flying well below Tolo and heading straight for him. Tolo laughed, and his face —he has a face like a young girl's—beamed with joy. A lone bomber is easy meat for a Hurricane.

His first attack in a steep head-on dive was unsuccessful. Evidently Tolo had failed in his aim in this difficult position. After passing the Dornier he pulled his machine up, and attacked again, from the back. First he splashed bullets over the fuselage and silenced the rear gunner. The bomber tried to escape by a desperate twist. In vain. Tolo put several bursts into the port engine. The engine began to smoke, not much at first, but soon more and more. And then followed a scene which filled the fighter pilot with awed amazement and silent rapture. The enemy began to dance his dance of death. A swan song waltzed all over the sky; the eccentric minuet of a mortally wounded madman.

First the German climbed up. In a great sweep, broad and gracious, like a pathetic flight from all earthly hazards. He seemed to soar endlessly. The higher he went the slower and more arduous was his ascent, until at length, at the end of his lofty arc, all his impetus was gone, and the plane paused in a theatrical gesture of doubt. A moment later he dropped down on the left wing, wavering, obviously swooning. Then he turned limply and went into a vertical dive. It seemed the expression of overwhelming lunacy as, tearing downward towards the earth's embrace, he wrote in the air his sentence of death. So he fell several thousand feet in a few seconds. But still death was not yet.

Halfway down to earth he pulled out from his dive and, turning away, missed death by the narrowest margin. Along an invisible hyperbolic line he rose again, with seemingly new life and strength, and having developed a fantastic speed, he climbed again to a fantastic height. He flew up to the zenith, to an absurdly sublime altitude

—both altitude and flier poignantly pathetic.

Tolo watched the bomber's evolutions with bated breath. Fighter pilots have a strongly developed sense of the beauty of movement. Aerobatics are the basis of their powers of defense, and aerobatics are a form of dance. They are an incessant improvisation, full of a grace which the pilots thoroughly appreciate. Tolo watched the unprecedented spectacle, first with delight and then with growing exaltation. He did not fire. There was no need to. He only flew aside and watched. His eyes drank in the charm of those inexpressible movements and reveled in their savage rapture.

But this lasted only a moment. Tolo was also a soldier, and his rapture was soon transformed to another pleasure, a soldier's pleasure. Here was a proud enemy who had come to kill and destroy and who everywhere had destroyed and killed, in Poland and elsewhere. And for him, a Polish pilot, this haughty foe was now dancing, the aberrant dance of an impotent witch. The enemy, powerless in his frenzy and fear, struggled and wrestled, unable to break the invisible net in which he had been caught. He had thought in his arrogance that he could rend the world and trample everything underfoot, but now—a wild beast hit by a spear and held on a magic cord— he danced like a madman, and in this delirious dance involuntarily did homage to his conqueror.

Tolo guessed what had happened: his fire had probably not only damaged one of the bomber's engines, but also seriously wounded the pilot who, still grasping the stick with convulsive hands, was transmitting the spasms of his agony to all the machine. Tolo kept the Dornier in sight and, with his imagination fully alive to all that he was witnessing, kept his thumb on the button, ready to fire another burst.

But there was no need for this precaution. It was the enemy's last fling, his final climb. After zooming up again to a deadpoint, the bomber slipped back tailfirst and fell into a back spin. One more dance from the zenith into the abyss, a long spiral of dizzy pirouettes, and then the end: he struck the water a few hundred yards from the shore, turned over on his nose and sank with his crew. The sea closed over him like a theater curtain.

The faithful of Mahomet make their pilgrimage

THE ENEMY'S DANSE MACABRE

to Mecca and dance as they go. The road to Poland is longer and still more toilsome than that to Mecca. It is winding, uneven, full of bypaths and thorns, yet honorable and frequently trodden in a dance. A dance of death. And somewhere along this road of a thousand turns, like a white milestone, stands the rocky coast of the English Channel, a mute witness of aerial dances and of the "303" fighter pilots' irresistible attraction towards "Frantisek's method."

13

A GALLANT CZECH, SERGEANT FRANTISEK

THIS DARING Czech was the exception among his countrymen: he was neither sober nor mannerly. In fact, he was altogether out of place in modern times; he had romantic exuberance and medieval fervor; he was like a volcano pouring out its lava in the least expected direction. He had his own ways and paths. There are few men like him nowadays. They either perish as criminals, or they become heroes. Frantisek became a hero.

When the Germans entered Prague in March 1939 he was one of the gallant few who actively protested against the aggression: he took up an airplane and flew it to Poland. He did this against the orders of his superiors and against what is generally called "common sense." He could have lived on quietly and peacefully in the

A GALLANT CZECH, SERGEANT FRANTISEK

Protectorate, like so many others. But he did not want to live in peace. He wanted to fight. He had to fight. His vital personality and his proud character were not made for life under aggressive totalitarianism and enslavement to Germans. Frantisek, true to his nature, flew to the country of future battles, and linked his fate with that of the Poles.

He went through all their sufferings. The tragic September and the road of retreat to Zaleszczyki, Rumania, the Balkan Odyssey. The Mediterranean and France. Always with them, always one of them. Not only because he was a kinsman and Slav, but because he, like them, was a resolute desperado. That was his strongest bond: together with the Poles he looked desperately for new weapons against the common enemy and for new battlefields. That united him with them.

They found both enemy and battlefields in France. Unfortunately the short-lived flame of France was hardly lighted before it died out. In that brief time, however, another flame shone out, the fame of Frantisek. An undying flame. He proved himself a superb pilot and a magnificent destroyer of Germans. In aerial battles over Belgium and Champagne he shot down ten German planes in three weeks. Then France collapsed; the weapons were struck from their hands again and they renewed their obstinate search to recover them. And so Bordeaux, the Bay of Biscay and Britain.

In Britain fate associated Frantisek with Squadron 303 once for all, in life and death. And above all in victorious battles. He took an outstanding part in all the Squadron's major encounters. From September 2nd onwards he scored new successes almost every day, and more than once he got two or three Germans at one take-off. He seldom returned without having added to his bag. He made a triumphant advance from victory to victory.

In one of the earlier battles there was an unpleasant incident. The leader of the section which included Frantisek all but lost his life through the sergeant's negligence. During an attack on several Messerschmitts the leader was dumbfounded at the last moment to find that Frantisek was not at his side. He had irresponsibly left the section on an expedition of his own. His defection frustrated the whole plan of attack

Swapping tales

Cherished respite

A GALLANT CZECH, SERGEANT FRANTISEK
and compelled the rest of the section to make a hasty withdrawal. When Frantisek returned to the station, it became known that after breaking away from the section he had shot down two Germans near Dover.

But when the same thing happened again and again during the next few days, the affair acquired a disturbing importance. Team discipline is a fundamental necessity in aerial combat. The commander of a section, squadron or wing must be able to rely on his fighters to carry out the task entrusted to them; otherwise there would be chaos and confusion. Frantisek was causing disorder.

After another of his lapses he was ordered to report to Squadron Leader Witur. Frantisek stood as taut as a bow-string. He always did: he was an extremely handsome young man, with bold eyes and an engaging swagger. He explained that he had seen a damned Hun some way off and couldn't control himself. He just had to go after him. He had been carried away. So he dashed off and shot down the Jerry.

"Sergeant Frantisek!" said Witur in his calm penetrating voice: "The Squadron is very glad to have such a splendid fighter pilot as you, but don't let us forget that we are soldiers, and that we must carry out our duty like soldiers. I insist that you are not to leave the formation before the battle."

"Very good, sir!"

His voice sounded quite sincere, and Frantisek was sincere when he spoke. For two days everything went well. But after that the devil again interfered, and Frantisek returned to his old habit. At 15,000 feet he became fidgety and at 18,000 feet the temptation was too strong for him. He vanished and went off over the Channel.

He felt happy over the coast. He waited there for the Germans who were bound to return that way from their raids over England. They usually returned in broken formation, often already mauled and always using the last of their fuel. They were easy prey. The English side of the Channel became the gateway to death for many a German.

"Frantisek's method"—as the squadron called this habit of hunting along the coast—found many adherents in the Squadron and also among British pilots. But there was one cardinal difference: the others went over the Channel after the battle and

A GALLANT CZECH, SERGEANT FRANTISEK
after carrying out their prescribed task. But although Frantisek often fought like them and with them, more often still he flew off to the coast immediately after he took off.

It was his passion, his mania, an irresistible instinct, an incurable disease. It was not merely ambition to put up his score; it was something more deeply embedded in Frantisek's mind and character. A jolly companion over the bottle, a good comrade at all times, a tender and generous lover—in the air he needed loneliness. There he could not bear company, he could not stand any restrictions, he burst all bonds. Up in the sky he was like the great eagles: lone, ferocious and jealous for their space. He did not want to share the air or his battles with anyone.

Frantisek's conduct undermined the discipline of the whole squadron. It presented an increasingly difficult problem for the commander. Must he exclude from the Squadron such an ace, who brought so much glory to his unit? It began to look as though that would have to be done, until the command found a solution worthy of Solomon, so sensible and so magnanimous was it: the Poles made the Czech sergeant a guest of the Squadron.

Of course guests are allowed many liberties. The advantages of this decision quickly became apparent, and his colleagues sighed with relief. And Frantisek? He reacted characteristically: the next day he shot down three Germans.

Once he had to land at another station in the south of England, and he told the British mechanics: "I am Polish!" Frantisek was no renegade, and he always considered himself a Czech. He used this phrase simply to indicate that he belonged to the Polish squadron and that he was body and soul with the Poles.

He was indeed one of them with all his heart. Their temperament most perfectly accorded with his own exuberant nature. The British, for whom he was a half-legendary figure, were delighted with him and did their utmost to get him to join one of their squadrons. But Frantisek remained indifferent to prospects of promotion and honors. He wanted to stay with the Poles, in their famous Squadron 303, and surprising to relate, he was not attracted even by the Czech fighter squadron which was then in the course of formation.

Frantisek was, of course, a supremely good

A GALLANT CZECH, SERGEANT FRANTISEK
pilot and marksman. He also had a marvellous presence of mind and a flashing speed of reaction. These qualities were once illustrated by an episode which occurred in full view of an R.A.F. station.

During one of the many combats over Kent, Frantisek harried a Messerschmitt 110 so effectively that the German signalled that he would surrender and land on the nearest airdrome. So Frantisek held his fire. The Messerschmitt lowered his undercarriage and glided over the airdrome. But it was only a ruse. His wheels were almost touching the ground when the German suddenly zoomed up on full throttle. He did not get far. Almost at the same moment Frantisek put such a burst of fire into him that he fell like a log and crashed on the airdrome—bringing new glory to the Sergeant.

Towards the end of September something began to go wrong with Frantisek's nervous system. The symptom was an extraordinary one: he was afraid of the ground. He went up more frequently than ever, for only high above the earth did he feel safe. On the ground he was oversensitive. During the German night raids he jumped up at the first warning and was the first to run to the shelter, though formerly he had laughed at such precautions.

His new mania possessed him as strongly as all his former crazes had done, and there was something truly moving, worthy of the deepest compassion, in the way this young daredevil, who took off against the enemy with the greatest of dash and the utmost sangfroid, was afraid of the earth when he returned to the safety of his base. He grew more and more panicstricken, as though for him the earth was a demon avenging itself on man for loving the air so unboundedly. In his passionate, impulsive soul, in the soul of the unusually fine fighter pilot, a profound tragedy was being played out to its final scene, which came a little later, on October 8th.

On that day, as Frantisek was landing on his airdrome after a fighting patrol, his wingtip caught against a hummock of ground and the machine was smashed. He perished with it. And so he died on the earth, as he had feared, one of the most outstanding aces of this war, Sergeant Josef Frantisek, who had shot down twenty-seven German machines, ten in France and seventeen in

A GALLANT CZECH, SERGEANT FRANTISEK
England. He held the Croix de Guerre, the Distinguished Flying Medal, the Polish Cross of Valor and Virtuti Militari.

He was an indomitable Czech who, when his own Motherland fell, sought a home in Poland, and who wanted to fight and who did fight only among Polish fighter pilots. In the final struggle with the hereditary foe, he and they showed how Poles and Czechs can stand together, shoulder to shoulder, actively and victoriously, and showed this long before the theoretical principles of the Czech-Polish alliance were drawn up around the diplomats' conference table.

14

THE GRAY ROOTS
OF BRILLIANT FLOWERS

Look into the heart of a fighter pilot, and you will find a great depth of feeling, not only, nor always, for his brother pilots, though they are all linked together by the common struggle and a common destiny. But you will always find the deepest of affection for the gray group of men who are known as the ground staff. The fighter pilot gives them his most intimate regard, he owes them more than he owes his pilot colleagues—his life, his victories, and his glory.

Also he owes them his boundless confidence in his machine. When a fighter pilot flings himself down on a couch in readiness for action, in his overalls and "Mae West," dozing until a telephone rings, he is amazingly calm and carefree. Above, in the vast, menacing space of the sky, the unknown awaits him. But the pilot is not afraid. For he feels strong. Strong in the knowledge that while he rests a ritual of duty and devotion is being performed around his airplane by the faithful mechanics. At the moment of take-off they will hand over a machine on which he can rely absolutely, and his confidence in the infallibility of his weapon carries him a long way towards victory.

When a fighter pilot returns after a successful encounter, he announces the good news to his mechanics with an audacious exhibition roll just over their heads. It is both a signal and a tribute to them. When a moment later he taxies over the runway, his upraised thumb and his laugh are meant for them. They get his first impressions of the battle and—strangely enough—it is they who feel the greatest pride, satisfaction and happiness. Just as though they had won the fight themselves. And with good reason: their machine has been victorious, the machine they have given life, which their hands have fed and cared for.

The pilot and his mechanics are filled by one common love for their machine. But their love is different: while the mechanics give all and get nothing in return, the pilot takes everything. He flies the airplane, he knows the glory of victory and collects the laurels. He is like a magnificent flower arousing public admiration, the subject of song, the recipient of honors, the caressed of the sun. The mechanics are like the flower's inconspicuous roots, truly necessary to its bloom, but unostentatious, in the shade, without the raptures and without the sun. Just gray roots.

There is probably no other fighting service in which these roots are so important as in the Air Force. When a pilot steps out of his fighter after a flight, he never worries about it at all until the next take-off, but leaves it in the hands of the mechanics. Now it is their turn: their devotion, their effort and their willing, but highly responsible service. They have to provide fresh ammunition, fuel, oil, glycol, to charge the oxygen tubes and to install new batteries; but that is not all: the complicated metal creature may be sick. A moment ago it was undergoing terrific stresses, exerting all the strength of its muscles—it may have suffered from the strain. It is subject, like humans, to mysterious complaints, treacherous and dangerous, worse than the open wounds inflicted by enemy bullets.

So the mechanic runs to the airplane with all the passion of devotion and gives it a thorough overhaul. He listens to its heart, fingers it, smells and penetrates to its vitals. He is no longer an ordinary soldier, a private or corporal, but a specialist of metal diseases, who knows that on his skill and thoroughness depends not only the pilot's life, but his victory in the next encounter. A squadron's victories are brought to birth on the ground, through the services of the mechanics.

The Polish pilots are worthily served by the Polish mechanics. Unsurpassable in their dexterity, far superior to those of many other nationalities, they give the lie to the legend that the Poles are only good farmers. Old Henry Ford had stressed the inventiveness of the Poles and described them as the most intelligent engineers in his works. And now once more they have passed the test. Like other Polish soldiers, they made their way across frontiers, went through the French campaign and finally landed in Britain. There, after only three weeks—a fantastic achievement—they had thoroughly mastered all the intricacies of the Hurricane and were servicing it as though they had known the machine for years.

It is an undeniable fact, definitely confirmed by the pilots themselves, that the remarkable successes achieved by Squadron 303 in September 1940 were due in large measure to its ground staff. To their courage, judgment, efficiency and devotion. There were days, nights and days, of incessant labor, without a moment of respite. There were cases of serious damage, which normally would have necessitated the machine's return to the works, but they dealt with it in the Squadron's own workshop. If the ground staff service had been only normal, Squadron 303 would have had to stop fighting about the middle of September for lack of machines. But "303" carried on without a single break. In spite of almost daily battles the full complement of twelve fighters was ready to take off every morning. That perhaps explains the Squadron's record. There were only four days when less than twelve Hurricanes were ready for action: on two days nine took off, on one day six, and the fourth was the memorable 15th of September.

Twelve machines went up at the first take-off on that day. At the second take-off there were nine, and at the third, towards the evening, only four. During the third flight no enemy airplanes were encountered: the *Luftwaffe* was already defeated and driven off. But at the end of that victorious day the Squadron's Hurricanes were in a piteous condition. Ten of them were unfit for flight. They had sustained all sorts of damage; control fins shot away, radiators smashed, control cables cut, wings and engine shields riddled, even the propellers had had a bad time. One machine had the main wing spar nearly broken at the junction with the fuselage.

The damage was clearly beyond the resources of the Squadron's repair shop. Yet the mechanics did not lose heart. It was expected that the enemy would return the following day in greater force than ever. The mechanics realized how much depended on them now. They went to work, and worked all night without being ordered: at such times orders are superfluous. It was not merely a matter of their personal ambition, but of the Squadron's very existence. They were exalted by an inspired frenzy; their fingers were winged; and they triumphed. The incredible, the impossible was achieved: at dawn of September 16th there were again twelve fighters ready to take off.

That day of glory for the British and Polish fighters had brought a night of glory for the Polish mechanics.

Their chief, Lieutenant Konkretny was one of the leading designers in the Polish aircraft industry before the war. He is the kindest of men, ever ready to help his neighbor, a good comrade, and also an excellent engineer and a fanatic for hard work. Work is his all-absorbing passion. His enthusiasm never flags. He has all the qualities to inspire others—and he does inspire them. It is difficult to estimate the services Konkretny rendered to Squadron 303; they are beyond all powers of appreciation. It is impossible to think of the victorious "303" without him and his staff of mechanics.

Yet the mechanics are only the gray, underground roots. Soldiers truly, but hardly of the first class. Before the war any self-confident but shortsighted infantryman, cavalryman or gunner looked down on them. Now it is different. The war has taught everyone to respect the mechanics. Views have changed, but not the spirit of the military regulations. According to their antiquated outlook the mechanics are still a kind of second-grade soldiers. Not for them are the honors. No Virtuti Militari or Cross of Valor for them.

These decorations are expressly granted for "valor in the presence of the enemy." But the air force stations must be situated as far as possible from the enemy positions if they are to carry out their task. In consequence the thousands who form the army of mechanics—every squadron has a ground staff from 150 to 200 men—can never fulfill this fundamental condition and are therefore ineligible for these distinctions. Owing to some regrettable misunderstanding they are deprived of this right, although on them depend the results of decisive battles, and on them, beyond all doubt, will depend the final victory in this gigantic war.

Not for them are the crosses and medals. Not for them—unless by unpardonable negligence someone blunders and allows the enemy to get over the airdrome. Not unless an enemy bomber unexpectedly appears and drops bombs among the mechanics. Then the requisite conditions are fulfilled. Then, for their self-control in a few moments of chaos, they can be decorated. But for their incessant devotion and toil, for the deadly efficiency of the air weapons, for their vital contribution to important victories, they get no recognition.

The military decorations—not only Polish, but those of other countries—were created in times when wars were decided literally by the sword, when hand-to-hand fighting was practically the only effective method of warfare. Although even in the present war hand-to-hand fighting remains an important factor in victory, it is no longer the only element; today there are others just as necessary and important.

The war front has developed a depth unknown to former staffs, and has penetrated hitherto undreamed domains, smashing the antiquated conceptions of military science. Even the conception of military virtue has undergone changes as revolutionary as those of strategy. In the old wars all that counted was dynamic courage, which found expression in hand-to-hand combat. In modern total war the fighting men are separated

Barring gremlins

Three United Nations

by thousands of tons of steel and are faced with new arsenals of powerful psychological weapons, which make potential courage as important for the final result as the traditional "conspicuous bravery in the presence of the enemy." There is such a thing as the courage of the war machine behind the front line.

Nobody denies that the staff officers of a victorious army are entitled to the highest military awards, if their work has contributed to the defeat of the enemy, even though they do their work far beyond the actual fighting line. The aircraft mechanics are in the same case; although working behind the line, they make an essential contribution to the defeat of the enemy, the importance of which it would be impossible to exaggerate.

And credit is due not to the mechanics alone, but to the entire ground staff. For it must be agreed that thanks to its speed and fire power a fighter squadron is a far stronger striking force than any brigade of 1914. If through its victories, as the Polish Commander in Chief said, Squadron 303 brought a glorious renown to the name of the Polish forces, it was only because every member of the Squadron showed and shows the utmost devotion in performing his duties. For the fighter pilots are helped to their victories, not only by the mechanics, but by the adjutant they call "daddy," by the doctor who picks up his wounded men all over the South of England, and by the officer in charge of the responsible task of operational control.

They all deserve our greatest gratitude. They deserve the highest distinctions: military honor and common justice demand it.

15

SANS PEUR
ET SANS REPROCHE

It is often said that the present aerial war does not produce aces, that it is mainly a war of teams. Certainly it is a contest of teams. Hundreds of airplanes take part in the battles of today, thousands will take-off tomorrow, and by the time the decision is in sight, it will depend on tens of thousands. All air battles are begun by teams. But the next moment the formations break up; individual fighters attack individual bombers or fighters. Then it becomes a hand-to-hand fight, and, paradoxically enough, the most modern of weapons, the airplane, reverts to medieval tactics in which a series of heroic duels decides the issue. In the air the stoutest personality wins, whether he be a sergeant or a colonel. The strongest alone can survive. And these supremely personal encounters bring out the supreme expression of fighter pilot qualities: the ace.

Certain pilots of Squadron 303, Dzidek, Paszko, Jan Donald, Ox, Szaposzka, Kar, Frantisek, are undoubtedly aces. Their high scores are not an accident. And it is no accident that the most outstanding of them all is Witur, who had a score of seventeen victories to his credit.

When you make his acquaintance you are faced with a problem. It is impossible to reduce him to any known standards; he is outside common human experience. He has all that the other fighter pilots have: a soldier's bearing, a strong face and a clear eye, but you feel that that is not all. You have a feeling of a new, hitherto unknown type of man, without precedent and unequalled. Then in a flash you see what it is: the man is metal. He is the definite personification of metal, of living steel. The gleam in his clear eyes, the ring of his voice, the buoyancy of his movements suggest aluminium, light yet strong. If aluminium were to acquire body and mind, the result would be Witur. No wonder that he and his fighter constitute a single, indivisible being.

Like most of the pilots in Squadron 303 he is

a professional soldier, a captain in the Polish army and a Squadron Leader in the R.A.F. His age is 34. He has a splendid record of devotion to duty in the grim September of 1939. As an instructor in the Air Training School on the outbreak of war, he received orders to take his group of fifty cadets to Rumania and train them there on French fighters. He crossed the frontier together with his pupils on September 17th, but as soon as his men were safe and in good hands he returned to Poland to take part in the fighting. Unfortunately, he was too late. He was taken prisoner by Soviet forces, escaped the night after his arrest, crossed the frontier again, and after three eventful days rejoined his cadets.

The weeks which followed were an Odyssey of fantastic stratagems, ruses, arrests and escapes, schemed and inspired by Witur. He finally achieved the almost impossible. He packed all his men into the bunkers of a vessel in Constanza. They sailed to Syria, then to France. There Witur, a model commander and indefatigable guardian, produced to the Polish authorities almost all his detachment—a highly valuable military contribution.

In January 1940 Witur was sent to Britain.

He shot down his first German in the middle of August of the same year, while still a member of a British squadron. That day he volunteered for flight and was flying as thirteenth at the tail of the squadron, guarding the rear of his companions. They were over the sea, near Portsmouth. The enemy was already over the harbor in front of them, when Witur noticed four Messerschmitts coming from behind—three on the right and one on the left hand—overtaking the squadron.

In his first encounter with the enemy, the pilot displayed his sound judgment and lightning speed of action. A false step could have had fatal consequences for himself and the rest of the squadron. But he took the only wise course: he first flew at the three Germans so furiously that he alarmed and dispersed them. Then he wheeled round to attack the fourth, who preferred to run away rather than fight.

A mad pursuit followed. Its climax came when the fugitive German rushed into a group of about fifty circling Messerschmitts with Witur after him. It all happened so quickly that none of them had time to attack the Hurricane, and in a flash the

German and Witur were through them. The German did his utmost to shake off the tenacious pursuer, but in vain. At last the eight guns found their target and the Hun crashed into the sea.

In that very first encounter Witur revealed the qualities which were so conspicuous in all his later successes: soundness of decision, speed of reaction, courage and vehemence.

Soon afterwards he joined Squadron 303, and when its commander, Squadron Leader Krol, suffered severe injuries in a burning machine, Witur took over the command of the squadron on September 5th. Squadron 303 was on the eve of its most glorious achievements, and with it Witur also won laurels. When in the second half of September the Germans were obviously flagging and the strain of the battle was beginning to tell heavily on both sides, Witur was just stretching his wings and getting into his stride, displaying his unusual stamina, his aluminium temper. And also the rapacity of a bird of prey. In three days, over a brief period, he shot down nine German airplanes. The last day, September 30th, especially had its epic moments.

On that day Witur led his squadron against

thirty German bombers over southern Kent and broke up their formation. He himself attacked a Dornier 215, which, slightly smoking, sought safety in a cloud. Then followed a game of hide and seek, and the Dornier made such skillful use of the clouds that it drew steadily away from the fighter. But over the Channel they ran into a zone of clear air, and then Witur quickly drew near to his maimed adversary.

But not far off he saw two Messerschmitt 109's, also returning to France. Although their presence there was quite accidental, they prevented Witur from finishing off the bomber. So he crept up behind the two Messerschmitts, who had no suspicion of his presence, until they were only 100 feet ahead. He came to such close range to make sure that they could not turn and make a direct attack: a long burst set the first on fire, and the other was also sent down before it knew what was happening. The way to the bomber was now open.

In the meantime the Dornier had approached the French coast and was flying lower. Witur was in pursuit, but he did not fire, for fear of wasting his last rounds of ammunition. He simply kept close behind his quarry, which was maneuvering desperately to dodge the blow. The rear gunner was silent, and evidently had already been put out of action. The Dornier was forced to resort to hedge-hopping, and tried to land in a field. A short burst from the guns of the Hurricane, and the bomber crashed and caught fire. Thus Witur destroyed his third German plane within a few minutes, bringing his total to seventeen.

When the squadron moved a few days afterwards to a second-line station for a rest, the British in their appreciation did not want to lose Witur even temporarily and attached him to the Fighter Group Command. Loyal recognition of services and the gift of making the best use of ability are the secret of British power and basis of their domination.

Witur is undoubtedly a fine example of the coming type of airman. It is an outstanding type. With simple, soldierly probity it absorbs the complex qualities of metal and creates a new alloy, healthy, strong, all-conquering, and by no means without human qualities. Vitalized aluminium, in which beats a living, human heart. Witur represents a positive type of the new mankind, and the British, conscious of this, have taken him to their hearts.

16

THE MYTH
OF THE MESSERSCHMITT 110

DURING THE early months of the war the Germans discreetly but effectively imbued the mind of the apprehensive world (and the no less alarmed Allies) with propaganda of the idea that they held in reserve a new, terrible surprise for the enemy in the form of a super-airplane, which was the height of inventive skill, the fighter machine *par excellence*. Something in the style of the Messerschmitt 109, but with a still higher ceiling, still greater speed, and an armament so powerful that it could destroy any enemy and remain fundamentally indestructible.

Few of these machines were used in the Polish campaign, and they were also very scarce over France. So the Allies had no very clear idea what the new machine was like, except that this Messerschmitt 110 was a heavily armed twin-engined fighter with a rear gunner.

However, in the Battle of Britain the *Luftwaffe* sent over a large number of Messerschmitt 110's, and showed their hand. The shroud of mystery was lifted, and the devil found it hard to live up to his reputation. After silencing the rear gunner, which proved to be a strangely simple matter, the devil could be taken by the horns and flung to the ground. And finally, one September day all the glory was dissipated, and the myth of invincibility burst like a bubble.

That day, over the eastern part of Sussex, Squadron 303 encountered a group of thirty German bombers, Heinkel 111's, flying towards London under a heavy escort of Messerschmitt 109's. The first two sections attacked the bombers, but the escorting Messerschmitts—and there were seventy of them—gave the Hurricanes a rough time. A furious battle developed. Fortunately other British squadrons arrived on the scene and helped to hold up the enemy.

Witur, who that day was leading the last section of the squadron, was attacked by several Messerschmitts, which he dodged again and again by violently banking. When at last he put his machine on an even keel, he found himself alone, far from the dog-fight. On one side he saw the German formation, which was just being attacked by fresh fighter squadrons, and on the other side, about 2000 yards to the west, he saw an amazing sight: a long, endless stream of aircraft flying in line from the south ahead towards London.

It was obviously another group of German raiders, flying parallel to the first. They were all twin-engined planes, and in the distance reminded Witur of the shapes of dive bombers. But approaching them rather closer, he realized that they were all Messerschmitt 110's. There were over forty of them, and evidently their task was to draw off the British fighters and thus enable the Heinkels to reach London.

As several other fighter machines came up to join Witur, they all attacked the head of the enemy's line. Instead of fighting, the long stream of German fighters simply coiled itself into a circle. It became a huge porcupine. All the Messerschmitts circled at the same height, thus forming a powerful aerial fortress, with considerable fire power in all directions. There seemed no way of getting to grips with it.

Witur and the other fighter pilots circled above the enemy, helplessly looking for a gap. Some of them tried to punch the deadly ring with short bursts, and then tore back. To little purpose. Two Hurricanes were already spinning down in smoke. Meantime the wheel continued calmly on its course, unbroken, challenging. In its confidence it seemed an insolent symbol of German arrogance, a ring of defiance, deriding the sky of England.

Witur soon realized that haphazard nibbling at the enemy would be useless. In the meantime other British fighters arrived on the scene, until they were nearly twenty in all. Witur reduced speed and dipped his wings. Five fighters responded to his sign and joined him. Diving down out of the sun, they fell on the nearest sector of the ring, with such good effect that three Messerschmitts were knocked out of the circle. This brought them within range of other Hurricanes. Two of them were immediately shot down, and the third fled with two Spitfires in pursuit.

The six attacking Hurricanes had scattered. Witur again climbed above the enemy ring, anxious to organize a second assault, but he was given no opportunity. Two Messerschmitt 109's dived down to cut him off.

Witur suddenly sees the yellow snouts aiming straight at him and an evil swarm of bluish trails. He dodges death by a violent turn, so violent that he half swoons, and though the consciousness of danger is still vivid in his mind, his eyes are sightless, and his head hangs limply. The horrible feeling of helplessness at this turning-point of life and battle is a nightmare which haunts the fighter pilot for ever after. . . .

In a few seconds Witur recovers his sight and sees a Messerschmitt 109 some 600 yards below him. But only one. The other has made off. The German has pulled out of the dive and is zooming up. Now is Witur's best chance: he steps on the gas, and attacks. The gunsight's red light, a press on the button; the German twists; the button again, another twist—then a spin. It is done. Less than half a minute ago the German was a strong man, full of hope and certain of victory. Now, hurled to the ground, he is no more. He is no longer an entity: his body is smashed to fragments. In their incalculable transitions from life's utmost exuberance to utter nothingness airmen live moments of demonic greatness, of terrifying exaltation. . . .

Witur climbed up again and returned to the Messerschmitt circus. Some changes had occurred during his absence. In the wheel, which was still revolving in the same spot, several machines were already beginning to smoke. But they still remained in the circle, and flying more slowly than the others, they left gaps in front of them. This was a bad omen for the Germans. Their ring was no longer perfect, its continuity was broken. The Hurricanes grew bolder, some of them too bold. Witur saw a British fighter which ventured too close: it was shot down, and the pilot baled out. But this did not affect the course of events. More Hurricanes and Spitfires were coming to join in the fun. The outer ring around the Germans grew continually stronger. Every minute the balance was more and more weighted against the Messerschmitts.

One of the German pilots lost his nerve, although he was not actually hit: he broke out of the circle

SQUADRON 303

with a sudden twist, and fled. Flying in the direction of France he went straight into the hands of Witur. Two Hurricanes gave chase. Witur, who was nearer than the others, dashed between the fugitive and the pursuing Hurricanes, so that they could not fire—and attacked. One burst from above and astern and another after pulling out of the dive. Still taking good care to keep the other Hurricanes out: this was his Jerry!

Suddenly the Messerschmitts swung round to fight. Witur zoomed up, turned on his back and raked the enemy's starboard engine and cabin with bullets. In his despair the Messerschmitt dived to try hedge-hopping. But a fourth attack sent him crashing to the ground, in sight of the two obstinate Hurricanes, stubbornly waiting for fortune to smile on them. They had no chance; they did not get the quarry; Witur settled the matter alone.

When the three returned to the circle, they found only half of the Messerschmitts, about a score, several of them smoking. They were still going round as though they were mad. The others, knocked out of the ring and shot down, littered the ground below. The Messerschmitt 110's not only had failed to carry out their task of diverting attention from the bombers (which meantime had been dispersed), but themselves fell into a deadly trap.

The twin engines and rear gunners were of no avail. Insolent pride had preceded a miserable defeat. Suddenly the whole ring collapsed like a rotten tree. The wheel was the fickle wheel of Fortune. The last of the Messerschmitts were chased like rabbits. The successful hunt was followed by a grand kill, and the hunters' tally-ho drowned the last echoes of the inglorious myth of the Messerschmitt 110.

This potent myth of a sinister mountain of predatory steel, a destructive volcano, had been built up in the heart of Europe. The present war is being waged to raze that mountain to the ground, to master its ferocity, to crush its steel and to disperse all such myths. The history of the present war will be measured by the stages at which the myths were shattered. One of the first to be blown sky-high was that of the Messerschmitt 110; perhaps the last will be the myth of the bloody demigod who proved to be an insane criminal.

That moment will mark the end of the war and the triumph of humanity.

17

STRATAGEMS

It is a grim paradox of the present conflict that the most brutal instincts of Teutonic barbarism have turned to their use the finest achievements of science and technical progress. The Messerschmitt 109 is the height of technique, a marvel of human ingenuity. But there are moments when it becomes a somber symbol of human perversion and monstrosity, for when this masterpiece of engineering fails and the pilot is threatened with death, he falls back into the twilight of history. At such moments of danger all the subtle achievements of military technique must give place to the naïve cunning of a Red Indian. . . .

A Messerschmitt 109 tried to attack the leader of a Squadron 303 section, Flying Officer Dzidek, from above and the rear, but it abandoned that

STRATAGEMS

design as soon as it saw Pilot Officer Jan Donald coming to the rescue. So the German contented himself with flying over the Poles and then turning right across the front of them, as though taking an insolent look at them. He was confident in his superior height and the proximity of other Messerschmitts; but he was overconfident and underestimated his opponents' eye and guns.

Jan Donald pulled up his machine slightly and fired a burst ahead of the Messerschmitt at a range of 300 yards, with plenty of correction. His calculation was perfect. The enemy flew across the field of death, began to smoke, and soon went spinning down, like a shot partridge. He dropped helplessly towards the ground, a victim of his own impudence.

"Good luck!" thought Donald cheerfully, and he made a mental note of the fifth German he had shot up that week.

Just as he was drawing alongside his leader he gave another casual glance at the falling enemy—and was flabbergasted. Donald is an ace fighter pilot, but he is also fiery and explosive in temperament: he swore like a trooper. A thousand yards below, the German who he thought was finished had pulled out of the spin and was flying along on a level keel, heading for France at full pelt. He was not even smoking any more.

"The artful dog!"

There was an ominous note in Donald's voice. Diving, he furiously gathered speed, swiftly overtaking the fugitive. When the German noticed his pursuer, he went into a spin again.

But he did not trick Donald this time. The Hurricane hung firmly on to the tail of the Messerschmitt and followed it down, firing again and again. Donald's bullets did not seem to have any effect—to hit an airplane in a spin is always sheer luck—but he went on firing with increasing impetuosity. Thus they dropped from 18,000 feet to 10,000.

Then Donald suddenly came to his senses: this was idiotic! If he carried on like this he would use up all his ammunition, and still not hit the enemy; then he might well become the Messerschmitt's victim. The German's seemingly naïve maneuver was in reality a cunning trap.

So Donald held his fire. He trailed the Messerschmitt, relentless and silent as a shadow, watching and waiting. Now he was very calm. He knew that there was no escape for the German, who must either pull out of the spin or crash on the ground. And if he did pull out . . .

The day was sunny enough, but clumps of clouds, like white islands, floated here and there. There were also small clouds a few hundred yards above the ground and, as the two fighters fell past them, the Messerschmitt again pulled out sharply from his spin. Was he intending to try one last trick and seek safety in the clouds? Nobody will ever know.

As soon as the Messerschmitt flattened out, Donald's guns went into action. Then the German unexpectedly did a roll—an amazing, useless evolution, often resorted to by German flyers at moments of danger. Donald had to pull up rapidly, to avoid a collision. He was back again in a flash, once more on the enemy's tail. Now the German neither wriggled nor fought. Donald gave him a few more bursts and finished him off properly, as though killing a mad beast.

This time there was no trickery or pretense: the Messerschmitt went down in flames. . . .

This was just an episode of the gigantic war, a minor incident, like thousands of others. The Messerschmitt's cunning did not save him. His stratagem failed.

When the time comes to settle accounts for the ghastly crimes which are being committed today against humanity, will the culprit not try to evade responsibility by some new trick? Will there be eyes keen enough to see through the game?

And all humanity, not only the other side, but we also, who have been drawn unwillingly into this collective lunacy—with what human values shall we pay for this lunacy, for the necessity to hate and destroy? For this tragic game of Red Indians?

18

HUMAN DESTINY
HANGS IN THE BALANCE

THE ENGLISH September is still strangely warm and mild. The sky is generously azure. The days seem to begin with a smile, as did the memorable Sunday of September 15th: when dawn dispersed the mists, small low clouds appeared in the sky and floated across it like swans, making the sunshine seem brighter than ever. It was a gracious, balmy day, and it was difficult to believe that against this background of pastoral beauty the most moving drama of all humanity was being enacted, that these delicate colors framed a somber picture of inexorable conflict and cataclysmic decision.

The Germans intended to bring the war to a climax on this day.

Their aerial attack on Britain had already lasted six weeks. Seventy main daylight raids had already struck at her centers of resistance. The Germans had certainly suffered serious losses, amounting to 1650 machines, but they were confident that they had inflicted even heavier casualties on their adversary. They had no doubt that the R.A.F. was straining its last resources and that the desperate population of Britain was preparing a revolution. That was one of the major errors made by the Germans in the present war. They were deceived by wishful thinking and blind arrogance.

But although they formed a wrong opinion of their enemy's condition, they knew their own strength perfectly: 200 divisions, victorious, invincible, which hitherto had crushed every enemy, every obstacle, waited impatiently on the Channel coast for the signal to invade, and thirsted for new conquests. Storm troops, already in their barges, gazed avidly at the white cliffs of Kent, watching on that Sunday for the first breach made by the *Luftwaffe*. Everything, the issue of the day and the issue of the world, depended on that first breach and on the success of the German airmen.

It is not yet possible to establish the number of German aircraft flung that day against Britain. Some authorities speak of over a thousand, but that is probably an exaggeration. The figure was very likely between 650 and 700. They came in several waves, of which the strongest were at noon and three hours later.

The first flight of Messerschmitts appeared in the sky soon after nine in the morning, spread fan-wise between the northern banks of the Thames estuary and Dungeness. They were patrols of moderate strength and their purpose was probably to draw the enemy out, to gauge his forces and cause uncertainty. But the Fighter Command quickly saw through the enemy's plan and did not allow themselves to be caught in the air.

Suddenly, shortly before midday, a large number of single- and twin-engined Messerschmitts appeared. They were flying very high at top speed, leaving behind them long white trails. These white bands, a common sight over Kent, were unmistakable in their menace: they traversed the sky like hostile arrows, all aimed at one target—London.

Although by now the Germans were in considerable force—several squadrons—the Fighter Command did not overrate its importance and made only a slight resistance, and the German fighters were allowed to penetrate deep inland. In other words, they were let through: a decision which had a favorable influence on the further development of events.

The battle which began a few minutes later again proved the valor and skill of the British and Allied fighter pilots, but even more it revealed the skill of the R.A.F. Fighter Command staff. A week earlier, on September 7th, staff work had failed, for the enemy in full force had reached the London docks in daylight. But now the whole action was dominated by a lively, dynamic and determined brain at headquarters. Not for a moment did it lose the initiative. The excellent network of observer and radio-location posts supplied accurate information about the enemy. All the movements of his formations were at once charted on the operations table. Against them the staff threw its fighter squadrons one after another, wisely, shrewdly and efficiently. There was a definite plan of defense, and every new situation was immediately tackled successfully. Somewhere in England, in the Fighter Command Headquarters, the entire genius of the Empire seemed to be concentrated, speeding the wings of its fighter squadrons with the will to victory.

A few minutes after the advance guard of Messerschmitts had penetrated into England, a new roar of engines, louder and deeper than before, was heard at Dover. A large force of raiders spread over the sky from the east: some forty bombers, mostly Heinkels, escorted by double their number of fighters. Immediately after crossing the coast, the bomber formation was attacked by two or three Spitfire squadrons. They worried them like fierce hounds. This attack was sharp enough to achieve the object desired by the British High Command: the Spitfires drew off most of the Messerschmitts, and the bombers flew on with a weakened fighter escort.

About twenty-five miles inland, halfway between the coast and London, the bombers encountered another, stronger force of Hurricanes, forming the second, main line of defense. Here the momentum of the German drive was broken. The raiders were compelled to accept battle, and were dispersed. In consequence they ceased to exist as an active, striking force. They broke up into scores of individual engagements, and were then defeated.

But it soon appeared that the Heinkels also were

merely preliminary to further action, for less than five minutes later a new, much stronger formation flew over. It consisted of some 150 planes, more than a third of them bombers. They struck England a hammer blow. Only now had the decisive moment arrived. A very real and urgent danger threatened the country. While the preceding waves had been sent only to fight, engage and exhaust the British fighters (already weakened, in the German opinion, by six weeks of battle), the new force was to obtain final mastery of the air over Britain. If only for a short time, an hour or two. If only long enough to drive in a wedge, which further invasion formations could follow up.

The huge raiding force crossed the coast like a tornado. It flew on unopposed. There were Spitfires in the air, but they were still fighting the Messerschmitts. The storm headed straight for London. Over Maidstone it entered the zone of the vast battle between the previous formation of raiders and the Hurricanes. The German armada passed around them and went on. It was almost clear of the zone when, to the Germans' surprise, new British fighter squadrons suddenly appeared in front. It was an unpleasant check. But the

German expedition had such an uncontrollable impetus that, although the British fighters struck at its ranks as if with murderous stilettos, they were able to hold and engage only half of the raiders; the rest, about 70 machines, tore on.

They reached London. The drone of German engines sounded over the town just as Big Ben was striking twelve. Among the raiding force were a number of bombers, but they did not do any great damage. They had no opportunity. Several new fighter squadrons, called up from other parts of England, arrived in the nick of time. They constituted a third, last line of defense, and their desperate blows shattered the enemy. Broken up and engaged in scores of dog-fights, the Germans had to flee. They turned for home, defeated.

The storm was over. The British Command had won. It had split up the enemy formations. The fighters did the rest. Over the vast stretch of sky between London and the Channel raged the strangest battle in human history. Two hundred furious duels were fought: it was a sight of fantastic beauty and whirling menace. The British fighter pilots knew what they were fighting for, and they fought like lions.

It is impossible to say what would have been the result if a fresh German expedition had appeared within that half-hour. Twenty British fighter squadrons were already engaged. There were presumably few reserves close at hand, since aid from other localities had been called upon earlier in the battle. But the German High Command did not rise to a new expedition. It was cowed, disabled, probably petrified by the unexpectedly strong resistance which had paralyzed all its elaborate plans. With no fresh supplies to replenish it, the flame over England burned out. Its dying fire brought success to Britain.

Squadron 303 fought magnificently in this vital battle. It won new victories, although it did not begin too well.

That day the squadron was led by Flight Lieutenant K., a daring but young pilot. Leading his twelve fighters over Tonbridge, he saw a group of some twenty Messerschmitts flying towards London. It was a tempting sight, and he gave chase together with his squadron. But the Messerschmitts were fast and difficult to overtake. K. was determined to get them. The Messerschmitts made a hardly perceptible turn northwards, de-

HUMAN DESTINY HANGS IN BALANCE

coyed the squadron over the Thames estuary and then returned over Kent, describing a huge circle.

Thus led by the nose, the squadron not only wasted many valuable minutes, but also scattered its formation over a great distance, and contact was lost between its own sections as well as with the enemy. When it returned to the battlefield it was flying in four separate sections of three fighters each. This was a serious disadvantage, but in these difficult conditions the Squadron 303 pilots once more demonstrated their outstanding skill as individual fighters.

The first section, led by Flight Lieut. K., went as far as Dungeness and boldly attacked a formation of over a dozen Messerschmitts. Flying Officer Ox and Sergeant Andrusz shot down two enemy machines from the very middle of the German formation, and then saved themselves from certain death by a desperate dive into the clouds. They escaped unhurt.

The second section, that of Flying Officer Dzidek, was attacked by Messerschmitts just as it was tearing into a formation of Dorniers, but escaped by scattering. Yet Jan Donald managed to destroy a "tricky" Messerschmitt, which tried to escape by going into an apparently helpless spinning dive. Meantime Dzidek single-handed tackled the bombers, which were heavily escorted. He set the first Dornier on fire, avoided the oncoming Messerschmitts by a swift dive under the bombers, and then attacked a further group of four Messerschmitts, bringing down one of them. He got away unscathed.

The third flight, led by Flying Officer Paszko, was also surprised and dispersed by several Messerschmitts, but Paszko engaged one of the attackers in combat and soon destroyed him. Pilot Officer Tolo evaded pursuit and saw a single Messerschmitt flying slowly away. It proved to be a decoy. As the Pole drew near and opened fire, other Messerschmitts dived down on him from above. One of their cannon shells shattered the side of his cockpit and wounded him. Tolo saved his life with a lightning dash into a cloud. But before disappearing, he had the pleasure of seeing the single decoy Messerschmitt go down in flames. He had given him only a short burst, but it was enough. Although Tolo had a badly damaged machine and innumerable splinters in his thigh, he took his machine back to his base and made a per-

Tallying up

Precious flower: comradeship

fect landing, to deliver his Hurricane to the repair shop and himself to the hospital.

The leader of the fourth section, Flying Officer Pis had on his right Sergeant Frantisek, who as usual flew off over the Channel and shot down a Messerschmitt 110. Pis chased a Messerschmitt 109, which avoided his fire by clever maneuvering and twisting. The German was so good at this game that he finally succeeded in slipping into a small cloud. Pis followed him and, of course, lost sight of the Messerschmitt at once. But the German's quickness of wit failed him in the cloud; he probably thought himself safe, and turned towards France. Pis divined his opponent's intention and turned in the same direction. When they flew out, Pis had the Hun straight ahead of him and shot him down easily with his first burst. In this game of hide and seek the two men had had the same idea. It had cost the German his life.

So Squadron 303, although scattered, did well. With its audacious courage—and audacity and courage were needed on that day—it kept busy a large number of Messerschmitts, enabling the other squadrons to fight the bombers. And, last but not least, Squadron 303 again had a record score that day. Although it was only one of the twenty R.A.F. squadrons, all of them straining every nerve to win, "303" destroyed nearly one sixth of the total shot down by all the other squadrons together. Its score was 9½ (for one German was shared with another squadron). A creditable result.

The British losses were small: less than a score of fighters lost and only a few pilots killed. Squadron 303 had a single casualty: one pilot wounded.

At Fighter Command operational headquarters Winston Churchill followed closely the progress of the battle, and—so it is said—let his cigar go out when the struggle was at its climax. A quarter of an hour later, about half-past twelve, he was already on his way home, cheerful and smiling. He and all the inhabitants of the British Isles sat down as usual to their Sunday dinner and ate it in a blessed peace.

A great page of history had just closed in their favor and in that of all humanity.

It will be a source of legitimate pride to the pilots of Squadron 303 to know that they helped to write that page of history, and wrote some of its most telling lines. Another Polish fighter squadron, the "302," also took part in the battle, and destroyed no less than 11 German machines.

But the day of September 15th was not yet over. . . .

19

THE BALANCE TIPS

The day of September 15th was not yet over.

The German barges were still waiting for the invasion signal. The way had to be cleared for them at any price. The British resistance had to be broken and the sky of Britain mastered, no matter what the cost in craft and men. "The last airplane will win!" Göring raged.

Within two hours of the midday defeat of the *Luftwaffe* German engines roared again over the Channel coast. The second attack that Sunday was as powerful as the first. It also came in two waves. The first was much the stronger. It was crushing. It wrote the most ominous signs in the sky, and embodied the Germans' fondest hopes.

Never before had so much been at stake in one throw: the fate of two thousand million living people, the fate of all the countries in the world, the fate of future generations. Never has so much of historical importance been crowded within a single hour.

Squadron 303 was sent up at 2.50 P.M. Only nine machines took off. The first flight of four was led by Flight-Lieut. K., the second, five machines, was commanded by Squadron Leader Witur. Immediately after taking off, operational headquarters wirelessed the order to take a south-eastern course, climbing to a height of 20,000 feet.

At 8000 feet the Squadron entered a heavy layer of cloud. It was perhaps a good screen for England, but it was inconvenient for the Squadron, for it hindered contact between the flights. The pilots of the second flight kept close to Witur like chickens to their mother. It was dangerous flying, with a continual risk of collision. To make matters worse the windscreens began to ice up, and were soon covered with a thick plate of ice. The nervous strain grew steadily greater, and with it the danger of catastrophe. But at last came the welcome dazzle of light: the squadron swept out above the clouds. Altitude: 22,000 feet. The layer of clouds below, three miles thick, was like a magnificent range of towering mountains.

The pilots looked about them for their colleagues, but in vain. They were alone, five of them, in that boundless ocean of whiteness and sunlight. The rest of the Squadron was lost in the clouds. There was nobody to be seen in the empty sky, either friend or foe.

The five flew on their appointed course, like lonely birds, continuing to climb. Ever higher, higher. The ice on the windscreens melted in the rays of the sun, and they could see again.

Suddenly they did see! Some three miles ahead small white balls were bursting in the sky. It was an anti-aircraft barrage firing through the clouds. In the distance it looked like a childish game, but the pilots were touched by the defiance of the gunners firing blindly through this dense ceiling of cloud.

And at the same moment they also saw the target, a bomber formation. Over sixty bombers, in compact groups of five, flying towards London, a few hundred yards above the clouds. Witur glanced at their serried ranks, recognized them as Dornier 215's, and instinctively, anxiously, looked for the German escort. Where was it? There! He had found it at last: flying a little behind the bombers and to their left, sunward. But they were extraordinarily, incredibly high, some 6000 feet above the Dorniers. It was a swarm of more than a hundred Messerschmitts, and the sky was nearly black with them. But why flying so high? The experienced pilot could not make it out, but he noticed that a few sections of three Messerschmitts each were circling below the high escort, between it and the bombers.

Suddenly, Witur's attention was attracted by five Messerschmitt 110's. They were flying in the same direction as the Polish flight, only six hundred yards to the left and a good deal higher. They were too near to allow of hesitation: Witur went after them. But almost at once he realized that it was a wild goose chase. Even flying flat out the Hurricane flight, forced to make height, could not catch the Germans. Witur's decision was reversed as quickly as it had been made. He chose a new target: the bombers.

The pursuit of the Messerschmitts had brought the flight within striking range of the bombers. They were ahead, to its left, several hundred yards below. The swarm of escorting Messerschmitts was almost directly above them, and glancing up, Witur all but choked with astonishment. Not one of them was diving down to attack. What a marvelous chance! The Messerschmitts were either ignoring the five Hurricanes—a mere speck compared with themselves—or else they simply had not noticed them from their high altitude. A remarkable turn of fortune had brought the Squadron 303 flight right into the middle of the unsuspecting enemy formation.

Witur swung sharply to the left. To attack. His colleagues understood him. They also turned and came into line abreast with him. All five dived together. At full throttle, at a dazzling speed. Thus only eagles strike. It was a mad race to win seconds: over the bombers scattered sections of Messerschmitts were still circling. They must be overtaken and passed in a flash. Witur missed nothing: about two thousand yards ahead of the bomber formation he saw two squadrons of British fighters approaching. In a few seconds the "303" pilots would not be alone. But they would be first. They were first.

They attacked three-quarters head on, from

above and coming from the sun. Straight on to the bombers. The bombers were flying huddled like a flock of sheep. The first bullets were fired at 400 yards. Well and shrewdly aimed: they were not concentrated in a long burst on one target, as is usual. Instead, each bomber was sprayed with short bursts. A slash here, a thrust there. One burst, then on to the next target. They riddled a dozen almost at once, and the whole left flank of the enemy formation was under fire. A terrific hail of bullets. The most effective and demoralizing of all.

How it happened will never be known: whether the accuracy of the Hurricanes' fire caused heavy casualties among the German crews, or whether the crews were confounded by the fact that the attack had come from the sun, where they had a powerful screen of Messerschmitts—the fact remains that the Germans lost their heads. The blow completely shattered them. They were seized with panic. The two nearest Dorniers crashed into each other and, entangled in a mass of wreckage, went rushing down. Whole sections on the flank swung violently to the left; others in the center tried to escape by diving.

The five fighters went right in to the attack: two of them raked the formation from top to bottom and bottom to top; the other three remained above the bombers. They dived, they fired down, looped the loop, then raked them again, shot them up again. Again and again: climbing, diving, firing. And so five fighters, raging in their element, transformed into death-spitting furies, made history: they smashed the whole great German formation.

The formation went to pieces. Now no power could bring it together again, no command could weld it into unity. Panic is a terrible thing. Even the bombers of the right-hand column, which had been least affected, turned tail and fled. They fled; but now fresh British fighter squadrons fell on them, attacked like new furies and spread more devastation.

At last the Messerschmitts struck from above. But they were too far off, they arrived too late. What though Sergeant Brzeza crashed down, plugged with bullets? And Sergeant Andro had his machine shot up and was forced to bale out? (And as he baled out he got caught by the wire of his earphones and was dragged horribly by the head for half a mile with the falling Hurricane, before he freed himself by tearing off his helmet.) What though Flying Officer Ox was attacked by a swarm of Messerschmitt 110's? In the mill he sent down one of them; then, with his machine damaged, he sought safety in the clouds. Down came the Messerschmitts, flying in from all sides. Scores of Messerschmitts! But they could not reverse the issue. They could not save the bombers from destruction.

The Hurricanes and Spitfires which also flew up did their job thoroughly. And among them that lucky pilot who had been the first to wade into the enemy: Witur.

At a certain stage in the fight he perceived three Dorniers profiting by the confusion to dive down through an opening in the clouds and get closer to the ground, probably to release their bombs. They slipped down one after another. Witur rushed after and overtook them. He flew around them like a wasp, striking and climbing. At the second attack the middle bomber was mortally hit. The next burst of fire disposed of the leading Dornier. The third (blast him!) prudently fled into the clouds. As he disappeared from Witur's sight the two other bombers were falling like shot ducks into the middle of the Thames estuary.

And once again, as three hours before, two hundred duels were fought out all over the sky. The Germans perished. Their machines went down. The *Luftwaffe* suffered its most crushing defeat. A total of 185 machines of theirs were destroyed that day, at midday and in the afternoon. Over two hundred more, badly shaken up, limped back to France. It was a decisive blow.

When on that 15th of September 1940, between three and three-thirty P.M., the remnants of the disintegrated Germans hurried back to France, the great battle known as the Battle of Britain was decided. Few of the British who sat down to their Sunday tea that afternoon were aware that a magnificent victory had been achieved. Still less did they realize that the fate of the second monstrous world war had been decided.

Never has a single hour been so pregnant with historic significance.

20

"WE ARE BEGINNING TO UNDERSTAND THE POLES"

The second half of September proved conclusively that the 15th of that month had brought the climax of the Battle of Britain and had decisively broken the German offensive. After that day the *Luftwaffe* could not muster any considerable strength. Its attacks lost their former vigor, and weakened. Even when at times they flared up in a final desperate fury, the British fighters invariably smashed them and exacted a heavy toll. For instance, on September 27th the R.A.F. destroyed 116 German aircraft, and Squadron 303 shot down fifteen. But this attack was the last flash in the pan.

Britain and the Empire were saved. Only the initiated knew how close Britain had been in that month to utter disaster: on land she had hardly any defense.

The Battle was won by the fighter pilots. They frustrated the German plan of invasion. On the decisive day twenty-one fighter squadrons shouldered the whole weight of the Teuton offensive and defended the entire might of the Empire. Even today, months afterwards, the very memory is breath-taking; it seems a terrifying fluke of history, an absurd paradox: the destinies of the 456,000,000 inhabitants of the British Empire depending on the valor and energy of about 250 pilots.

Thin was the thread which bound the British Empire together during those days, yet it did not break. By standing the strain, it aroused the conscience of the world. Only when, by an almost superhuman effort, these "few" achieved their task, were the rest of the Empire and the United States of North America awakened to the true meaning of this war.

It was a narrow front that the two hundred and fifty men defended, but how far-reaching in its consequences. It rendered possible the formation of a wider world front, stretching from Washington, through London and Moscow to Chungking. And only an armed force drawn from all over the world will destroy the German hydra. But in

"UNDERSTANDING THE POLES"

those months of August and September there were only a handful of defenders.

Among those few were also Poles. And the Poles included Squadron 303. Its contribution to the Battle of Britain, in its most vital stage, during September, was undoubtedly magnificent. Its bag of Germans shot down was three times as high as the average of all the other squadrons. Yet its losses were only one-third of the average.

Expressed in figures, the achievements of the Polish fighter machines in all squadrons, and those in the R.A.F., during September 1940 were as follows:

SQUADRON 303: 77 Germans shot down by Poles, 17 by the Czech, Frantisek, and 14 by the three British members of the squadron. A total of 108 shot down in September. For the entire period of the Battle of Britain the squadron had a total bag of 126.

SQUADRON 302: 19½ Germans shot down in September, and 26½ during the Battle of Britain. (The squadron came into action rather later than "303.")

Other Polish fighter pilots, assigned to British

units, shot down 21 Germans in September, and 89 during the Battle of Britain.

Total of Polish successes in September: 117½ Germans shot down. The rest of the Royal Air Force accounted for 846½ Germans (Ronald Walker: *Flight to Victory.*) Thus the ratio of Polish successes to the rest was 1: 7.2. It must be added, to complete the picture, that anti-aircraft artillery accounted for 131 machines in September.

A comparison of achievements on the vital day of September 15th is still more favorable to the Polish pilots. For on that day the two squadrons, i.e., "303" (14 Polish successes, 1 British, 1 Czech) and "302" (11 successes), together had 25 Polish successes, while other pilots had 153 Germans to their credit. Thus the ratio of Polish to other successes on that day was 1: 6.1.

So it is not surprising that the Polish fighter pilots are known by their achievements all over Britain. It is not surprising that the Polish Commander in Chief visited Squadron 303 to decorate its members, and the King himself came to shake hands with them. British writers also have appreciated their merit. George Saunders, the au-

Raring to go

Like other men . . . laughs

"UNDERSTANDING THE POLES"

thor of a best-seller of 1941, *The Battle of Britain*, wrote:

". . . Conspicuous among them are the Poles. Their valor is tremendous; their skill bordering on the inhuman. They have done great service. They are still doing it, and they will go on doing it until victory, triumphant and complete, lights up their wings. We are beginning to understand the Poles. . . ."

What, you may ask, are the famous pilots of Squadron 303 really like? Are they supermen? Are they a team picked for exhibition purposes, a national symbol? Are they prodigies, freak performers? That is just what they are not. They are ordinary, healthy, simple boys. They have the same temperament and mentality, the same smile and the same cares as most other Poles; they are just like thousands of other people living along the Vistula, the Warta, the Bug or the Dniester; they are neither better nor worse than the rest. They simply learned their job thoroughly in the old Polish school and are now conscientiously doing their duty—and that is all their secret.

That the efficiency and achievements of Squadron 303 are not exceptional is confirmed by the performance of other Polish pilots in British R.A.F. squadrons, and by the results obtained by the Polish Squadron 302. The pilots of "302" even have a record of their own, for they managed to bring down altogether 26½ German machines, although they were stationed far from the main field of battle. When they got a chance of meeting the enemy in force, as on September 15th, they showed up well, destroying 11 Germans.

The story of the Polish airmen in Britain had its element of tragedy, itself a reflection of Poland's tragedy. Even the most fair-minded foreign nations are inclined to form very peculiar, sometimes fantastic, views about the Poles. The position of Poland is about the worst in the world, between two insatiable powers, employing the most ruthless propaganda machines. For this reason information about Poland is often inaccurate and biased. (One small example is the use in British atlases of German names and terms for Polish towns and places, as for example Posen, Lemberg, "Polish Corridor," etc.)

In the summer of 1940 some circles of the R.A.F.

"UNDERSTANDING THE POLES"

Command, conscious of their tremendous responsibility, were doubtful about the employment of Polish pilots in the defense of Britain. They took the view that after two defeats the Poles would lack the morale necessary for fighting on such a vital sector. When the Poles were brought into active service they quickly proved that this view was not exactly correct.

Later the opinion was common that the Poles gained such great successes because they are mad dare-devils, heedless of their own life. That also was hardly correct, for during the Battle of Britain the Polish casualties were relatively much lower than those of other pilots.

"The Poles are only good as fighter pilots, because they have such a mercurial temperament!" This widespread judgment also had to be modified when more and more Polish bomber crews distinguished themselves by their efficiency and whole-hearted seconding of their British colleagues.

"The Poles are only landsmen!" This also was said at one time, but the achievements of the Polish submarines and other naval vessels, such as the "Orzel," the "Blyskawica" and "Grom," and the effective daily work of the Polish merchant navy, have disposed of that misconception.

The Germans have always declared and still declare (and the world has always been inclined to believe them) that the Poles are an unruly nation, incapable of creative work and organized effort. But within ten years of the recovery of Polish independence the small fishing hamlet of Gdynia grew into the largest port on the Baltic, with a turnover surpassing that of Stettin, Stockholm or Leningrad, and in the south of Poland a new Central Industrial Region was developing at a remarkable rate, until the Germans laid their hands on it.

Poland's near neighbor has for years been telling the world that the Poles are a nation of reactionary landlords and romantic, arrogant aristocrats. Yet Poland's social and labor legislation was perhaps the most liberal and comprehensive in Europe.

A nation of aristocrats. Nearly all the Polish airmen fighting in Britain are sons of the middle and laboring classes.

If the Polish airmen were asked what Great Britain owes them for their services in this country and how the debt is to be paid—perhaps a tactless, but still a very human question—they would look surprised and would probably retort that they were carrying out their duty as loyal allies, and expected no reward.

On second thoughts, however, they might ask for a reward. They would ask the British people to get to know the Poles better. To know them honestly, intimately, through and through, putting aside prejudices and preconceptions; to know the Poles as they really are and not as their neighbors represent them.

Then the British would no doubt discover that the nation living on the banks of the Vistula is just like all the other healthy and civilized nations, neither better nor worse. They would find that the average Pole is not very different from the average Mr. Brown of London, Mr. Bruce of Edinburgh or Mr. Taylor of Chicago. He believes in the same immutable moral standards as they do, will keep his word and never become a Quisling.

And since the Poles are not different from other decent nations, after the war they can be of great service to humanity, not by making exalted declarations and expressing high-flown aspirations, but through practical achievement. Just as the Polish airmen have served Britain during the most vital month of her existence. Provided always that their fate is not decided by people who do not know and understand them.

That is the reward which the Polish airmen desire: a fair and intelligent view of their nation.

who return   the date due rend

SALVAGE